Battle Orders • 33

The US Army in the Vietnam War 1965–73

Gordon L Rottman

Consultant Editor Dr Duncan Anderson • *Series editors* Marcus Cowper and Nikolai Bogdanovic

First published in Great Britain in 2008 by Osprey Publishing,
PO Box 883, Oxford, OX1 9PL, UK
PO Box 3985, New York, NY 10185-3985, USA
Email: info@ospreypublishing.com

Osprey Publishing is part of the Osprey Group.

Transferred to digital print on demand 2014

First published 2008
2nd impression 2008

Printed and bound in Great Britain.

A CIP catalogue record for this book is available from the
British Library

ISBN: 978 1 84603 239 4

Editorial by Ilios Publishing, Oxford, UK
(www.iliospublishing.com)
Design by Bounford.com
Index by Alan Thatcher
Originated by United Graphic Pte Ltd., Singapore
Typeset in GillSans and Stone Serif

Author's note

The author is indebted to Joe Trevithick, Lynne Black, Shelby
Stanton, Stéphane Moutin-Luyet, Steve Sherman of RADIX
Press, and Yves J. Bellanger for their assistance.

The Woodland Trust

Osprey Publishing is supporting the Woodland Trust,
the UK's leading woodland conservation charity, by funding
the dedication of trees.

www.ospreypublishing.com

MIX
Paper from
responsible sources
FSC® C013604

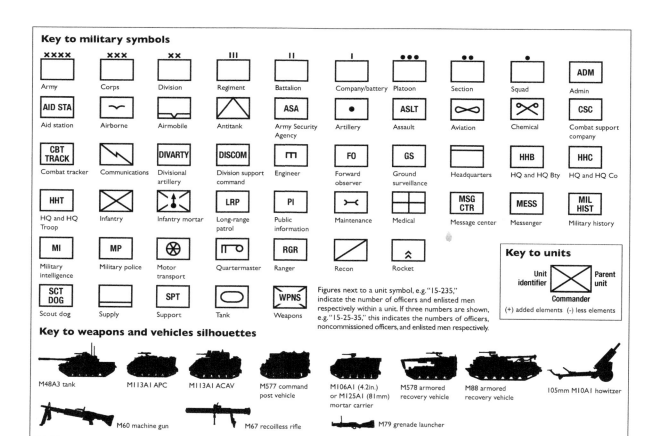

Contents

Introduction

The seminal book on the organization of the US Army in Vietnam is Shelby Stanton's *Vietnam Order of Battle: A Complete Illustrated Reference to U.S. Army Combat and Support Forces in Vietnam 1961–1973*. This extremely detailed tome examines all echelons of organization in units deployed to Vietnam during the course of a lengthy war. It provides the dates of arrival and departure, strengths, function, and assignment of every unit down to battalion level. It also lists all company-level units and order of battle of the US Army in Vietnam.

This more modest work is designed as a companion and focuses on the small-unit level, battalion and below, although divisions and brigades are not neglected. How each deployed to Vietnam is discussed along with its missions, where it fought, and when it returned home. Units in Vietnam were more often than not understrength, and this had a major impact on how units were internally organized and how they were employed. US Army units were organized and equipped for a conventional war, and even a nuclear war, in Europe in an armor and mechanized environment. The Army, however, recognized that it could be called upon to deploy forces in lower-level conflicts anywhere in the world. The specter of counterinsurgency operations and unconventional warfare was recognized, though not fully understood, as evidenced by the fact that many of the heavier weapons assigned to units were inappropriate or unnecessary for the type of fighting experienced in Vietnam.

Much of Vietnam was densely forested. It was not truly jungle in many cases, but to the soldier on the ground it made no difference what it was called. Visibility was often limited to 3–30m (10–30ft).

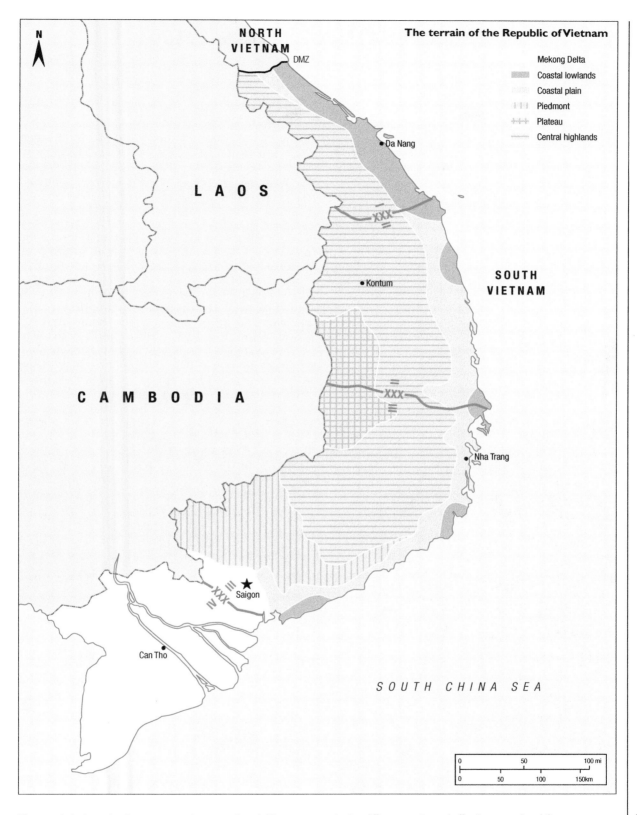

The terrain had a major impact on combat operations in Vietnam, necessitating different tactics and affecting ground mobility.

Combat mission

The US Army's role in Vietnam was to establish a safe environment within which the people of South Vietnam could form a government that was independent, stable, and freely elected – one that would deserve and receive popular support. The Viet Cong (VC) and the North Vietnamese Army (NVA) occupied or controlled, to some degree, large parts of the country and subjected many areas to armed attacks and terrorism. Terrorism and assignations were mainly directed at government representatives in villages and hamlets as well as at provincial and district-level officials.

The US military goal was to establish a secure environment free from enemy exploitation, pressure, and violence and to allow the legal government to function. US strategy to achieve this goal consisted of three independent elements: the ground and air campaign in South Vietnam, the nation-building effort in South Vietnam, and the naval and air offensive against North Vietnam. These efforts strove to convince the Hanoi regime that its aggression could not succeed and would be too costly to sustain.

The US Army mission was to conduct aggressive combat operations focusing on NVA and VC Main Force units, destroying them by fire and maneuver, disrupting their logistics, and supporting and advising the Army of the Republic of Vietnam (ARVN) forces. They were also to assist the Vietnamese people in secure areas with construction, sanitation, and medical care.

Vietnam is often considered a guerrilla war. Guerrillas played an important role, although this diminished as the fighting wore on. VC elements were

There were also large open areas in Vietnam. Here a distant tree line facing a firebase is covered by a .50cal M55 quad machine gun mounted on a firing platform rather than its usual 2¹/₂-ton truck.

scattered unevenly throughout the country depending on the degree of government control and the value of its resources (people, food supplies) to the VC. VC Main Force and regular NVA units operated out of Laos and Cambodia – privileged sanctuaries – thrusting into South Vietnam in efforts to seize key cities and areas. While they might be found in any area, they were most active in the northern provinces of I CTZ (Corps Tactical Zone), in the Central Highlands of II CTZ, and throughout III CTZ, focusing on securing a route to Saigon. They were seldom seen in IV CTZ's Mekong Delta. These Main Force and NVA units were not guerrillas by any stretch of the imagination. They were light conventional forces. They were supported by local guerrillas (scouts, guides, porters, local security, food supply, and others) and may have used guerrilla-like tactics and techniques when necessary. However, they conducted regimental, divisional, and multidivisional operations intended to directly attack and destroy Free World Forces and seize population centers. They may have lacked air support and tanks, employed mortars and rockets instead of tube artillery, used only light antiaircraft weapons, and had an extremely lean logistics tail, but that was out of necessity. This was dictated by the rugged terrain, the Free World Force's control of the road network, the Main Force and NVA need to rapidly travel through concealing countryside owing to Free World domination of the sky, and the allies' ability to rapidly deploy and sustain troops by helicopter.

The changing climate made the rugged terrain worse. Here a medic trudges through a sea of mud during the monsoon season.

It was a war of attrition, and, unfortunately, the Army began to focus on body counts to show a means of success in the absence of set-piece battles defeating large forces, liberating cities, and indicating that a clear-cut victory was in sight. Instead, it was a war against a shadowy, elusive enemy, misunderstood as a civil war, being fought among an often indifferent civilian population that suffered more than the soldiers.

The seemingly unending war's long duration, the weakening of the overall Army, increasing opposition at home, weak-willed politicians, and the disintegration of unit cohesion – owing to the 365-day individual rotation policy – coupled with increasing racism and drug problems, eventually degraded the Army to a shadow of its former self. The one-year rotation policy is often debated. It was a morale boost to individuals because they knew how long they would be deployed, but it made a shambles of unit cohesion. It did not require a year before the originally deploying unit was turned over. Within about five months, a unit was composed of about 50 percent replacements, owing to casualties, injuries, illness, and transfers. After that it was a constant exchange of experienced troops for green replacements – to include leaders.

The Army was also hampered by its own conflicting view of the war. It attempted to conduct a counterinsurgency that involved large conventional forces to "win the hearts and minds" of the people, while often being forced to destroy their homes and relocate them to secure areas. Furthermore, the Army could not effectively attack the enemy's logistics infrastructure in neighboring privileged sanctuaries.

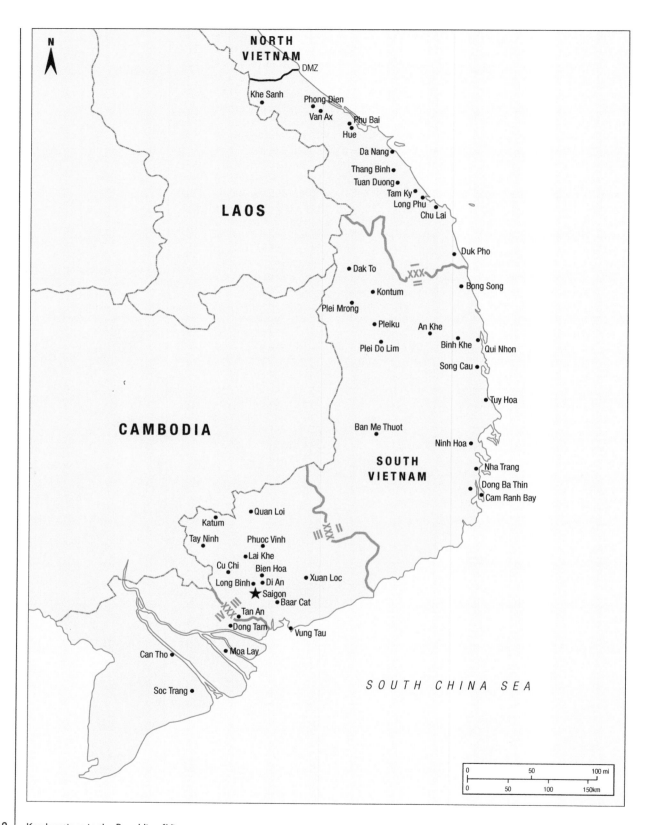

Key locations in the Republic of Vietnam.

The Army, organized, armed, and trained for conventional and even nuclear wars in Europe and Korea, did have a counterinsurgency doctrine. It issued manuals on guerrilla warfare, counterinsurgency forces, jungle operations, and related operations. They sometimes used earlier, successful counterinsurgency wars as models, but these did not always fit the circumstances in Vietnam. The Army would have to adapt its organization, tactics, techniques, and employment of weapons to Vietnam.

While the authorized strength and equipment according to Tables of Organization and Equipment (TO&Es) is listed in this work, the reality was vastly different, and TO&Es had little meaning. Units were habitually understrength with shortages of officers, NCOs, and specialists particularly common. It was not unusual for rifle companies to be as low as 50 percent strength. The allocation and employment of weapons and vehicles were often much different than that found in the TO&Es. Some weapons were withdrawn, especially recoilless rifles, and mortars were reduced. Other types of weapon were increased.

Manpower shortages were caused by the individual one-year duty tour rather than replacing units; the requirement for 25 months between tours; the need to maintain forces in Germany, Korea, and other overseas stations; and the political decision not to extend the active duty tours of conscripted troops and Reserve officers and not to call up and deploy National Guard and Reserve units, except in very limited numbers.

Another factor was the various restrictions that made troops ineligible for deployment: the 25-month redeployment restriction, less than two months remaining on an enlistment, sole surviving sons, soldiers under 18 years of age, physical restrictions from previous wounds/injuries, pending judicial actions, and rare family hardship waivers.

US Army ground combat units entered Vietnam in May 1965 to find themselves fighting a different kind of war than that for which they had been trained. However, they did not enter blindly. For years, large numbers of Army officers and NCOs had been serving as advisers with the ARVN. They already knew that it was a war without front lines – a war of ambushes and small unit actions – and that infantry units would have to rely largely on foot movement on difficult terrain and that helicopters would play a key role.

Unit organization

The focus of this book is on the units that bore the brunt of the ground fighting in Vietnam – the infantry and tank battalions, armored cavalry squadrons, and artillery battalions. This is certainly not to discredit the many other types of support units. They were equally important.

Organizational principles

The basic Army tactical structure was a named or numbered theater army with one to four corps – two or more divisions per corps. Divisions consisted of three brigades, each with two to five maneuver battalions plus division artillery, division support command, and division combat support units. Battalions consisted of a headquarters unit and two to five company-sized units. Battalion-sized armored cavalry and air cavalry units were designated squadrons that were composed of company-sized troops. In the artillery, company-sized units were called batteries.

Brigades consisted of a varied number of battalions and support units. A group was the equivalent to a regiment with regard to echelon, but it was composed of a varied number and type of attached battalions and companies. Groups were support units tailored to accomplish their mission. Only one actual regiment served in Vietnam, the 11th Armored Cavalry Regiment (ACR). It had a fixed organization and was considered a tactical brigade-equivalent command.

Organizationally, there were two types of battalions. "Fixed battalions" had a headquarters unit and a prescribed number of organic company-sized units permanently assigned to the battalion and designated by letters (A–D, for example). This included both combat and support/service units. A "flexible battalion's" only organic unit was its headquarters. Separate numbered support/service companies and detachments of different types were attached to the battalion to tailor it for its mission. Any type of support/service unit could be augmented by specialized "cellular units." Their TO&E designated them as a "team" identified by letters. Examples are a Team FA, Civil Affairs Language (two men) and Team NB, Signal Crypto Support Type B (21 men). There were scores of different types of these building-block teams that could be assigned to a unit to tailor it for its mission.

A detachment was a unit of fewer than 80 men but administered as a company, a "separate reporting unit." Some types of detachment operated as separate units attached to divisions and brigades with specialized capabilities, such as chemical or military intelligence detachments. Other types were absorbed into support units and lost their identity as a unit. There were also separate specialized platoons, such as infantry scout dog platoons, attached to units in the same manner.

The organization of headquarters units must be understood. Every Army unit and organization from

US Army Ranks		
Rank	Abbreviation	Pay grade
Private 1	PV1	E1
Private 2	PV2	E2
Private first class	PFC	E3
Specialist 4	SP4	E4
Corporal	CPL	E4
Specialist 5	SP5	E5
Sergeant	SGT	E5
Specialist 6	SP6	E6
Staff sergeant	SSG	E6
Specialist 7	SP7	E7
Sergeant first class	SFC	E7
Platoon sergeant	PSG	E7
Master sergeant	MSG	E8
First sergeant	1SG	E8
Sergeant major	SGM	E9
Command sergeant major*	CSM	E9
Warrant officer 1	WO1	W1
Chief warrant officer 2	CW2	W2
Chief warrant officer 3	CW3	W3
Chief warrant officer 4	CW4	W4
2nd lieutenant	2LT	O1
1st lieutenant	1LT	O2
Captain	CPT	O3
Major	MAJ	O4
Lieutenant colonel	LTC	O5
Colonel	COL	O6
Brigadier general	BG	O7
Major general	MG	O8
Lieutenant general	LTG	O9
General	GEN	O10

Note:
* CSM introduced May 28, 1968.

battalion up had a headquarters and headquarters company (HHC, or "head and head"). There was even an HHC, Department of the Army. Some types of unit, usually specialized battalions and groups, had a smaller headquarters and headquarters detachment (HHD). Artillery units had a headquarters and headquarters and service battery (HHSB). Armored cavalry and air cavalry squadrons and regiments had a headquarters and headquarters troop (HHT). Some service support battalions had a headquarters and headquarters and service company (HHSC). The "headquarters" was separate from the "headquarters company," being composed of the commanding officer (CO), executive officer (XO), principal staff officers, and the sergeant major. The headquarters company itself had a company headquarters, a battalion headquarters section with assistant staff officers, noncommissioned officers (NCOs) and enlisted men (EM), plus a number of platoons and sections that provided administrative and service support (communications, supply, transport, mess, maintenance, medical, among others). Brigade and higher headquarters companies were composed mostly of only specialized staff and administrative sections.

The formation of provisional companies and battalions was common. These temporary units were formed (not activated) by employing personnel and equipment taken from other units. The personnel were still charged to their assigned unit for accountability, administration, and discipline. Such units were formed to fulfill a special need or to provide additional units of this type owing to a lack of officially constituted units. Once their requirement had passed, they were disbanded (not inactivated), but, in some instances, their assets were used to organize an officially constituted unit. However, that does not mean the provisional units were "redesignated" as the new units. Officially constituted units do not carry the "lineages" of provisional units.

Unit designation practices

Divisions in Vietnam were numbered in the infantry division sequence, regardless of type (including airborne), dating from World War I. One oddity was the two airmobile divisions, 1st Cavalry (Airmobile) and 101st Airborne (Airmobile).[1] At the end of his tenure as Chief of Staff of the Army, Gen Harold Johnson's last act was to redesignate them the "1st and 101st Air Cavalry Divisions" on June 27, 1968. One of Gen Westmoreland's first acts when he took over the office was to restore their proper designations on August 26. As such, the name change is not even addressed in unit lineages. Divisional brigades were numbered 1st–3rd Brigade followed by the division designation, e.g., 1st Bde, 1st InfDiv, and no branch or functional designation was included. Separate brigades included branch and functional designations as did group designations.

Noncombat arms battalions and separate companies were designated in sequence within their branch, a series dating from World War II or earlier. Branch designations were included with the functional designation followed in parentheses, e.g., 307th Signal Battalion (Support) or 242nd Aviation Company (Medium Helicopter).

Combat arms branches include infantry, armor, artillery, and certain engineer and aviation units. Some infantry and armor battalions carried "cavalry" designations, but this was only a traditional designation. Armored cavalry and air cavalry units were armor branch units as well, with cavalry being a traditional designation and no longer a branch. Aviation was not a branch either; aviation units were assigned to infantry, armor, artillery, transportation, medical, military intelligence, and other branches. The artillery branch included both field artillery and air defense artillery, but both types of units were designated "Artillery." On December 1, 1968, the artillery was split into two branches, field artillery and air defense artillery. However, units were

---

1 At one point, it was going to be designated the 101st Infantry Division (Airmobile).

A rifle squad pauses before venturing into a bamboo grove. Squads were typically far under their authorized ten-man strength, but they usually had an M60 machine gun attached. Squads were as small as five to seven men.

not redesignated as such until September 1, 1971. Infantry, armor, and artillery unit designations were governed by the Combat Arms Regimental System (CARS) adopted in 1957.

With the elimination of the regiment as a tactical unit, a means of preserving the lineages of company- and battalion-sized units, as well as regimental histories, was necessary. The regiment was only a paper organization providing its historical lineage to combat arms battalions and separate companies; it did not exist as an echelon of command. The original regiment's 12 companies (A–M; there was no Company J) and the three battalion HHCs provided the lineages for battalions and separate companies with the new battalion's HHC carrying the original company's lineage and its own organic companies beginning new lineages. These battalions and separate companies might be assigned to different divisions and commands or they might all be in the same division.

An example can be found in the 50th Infantry. HHC, 1st and 2nd Battalions (Mechanized), 50th Infantry carried the lineages of the Companies A and B of

The M113A1 armored personnel carrier, or simply the "track," was provided to each mechanized rifle squad and was used in headquarters and support units. The "one-one-three" was armed with a .50cal M2 machine gun. The rifle squad also possessed an M60 machine gun without a dedicated gunner, which might be mounted on the track at the top cargo hatch.

M48A3 tanks were also used as mobile pillboxes for firebase defense or for securing road intersections, a role hated by armor officers.

the original 50th Infantry while those battalions' Companies A–C had new lineages. In other words, the modern Company A, 1st Battalion, 50th Infantry did not carry the lineage of the World War II Company A – the battalion did. The 1st Battalion was attached to the 173rd AbnBde in Vietnam, and the 2nd Battalion was attached to the 2nd ArmdDiv in the States, from which the 1st Battalion had been detached. There was also Company F (Long-Range Patrol), 50th Infantry, which carried the line of the original regiment's Company F, 2nd Battalion but had no association with the modern 2nd Battalion. Note that "Regiment" was *not* included in the designation. The infantry battalions of the 1st CavDiv (Ambl) were designated "Cavalry" for traditional reasons but were still infantry units and did not use troop and squadron designations, e.g., Company A, 1st Battalion (Ambl), 7th Cavalry.

Fixed battalions had lettered companies/batteries designated A and upward. In infantry battalions, the three rifle companies were A–C, and, if it had a combat support company (CSC), it might be designated Company D or CSC. When fourth rifle companies were assigned to battalions in Vietnam, the rifle

Armored cavalry units began replacing their Patton tanks with the M551 Sheridan armored reconnaissance airborne assault vehicle in late 1967. It was armed with a 152mm gun.

The 81mm M29A1 mortar saw little use in the field owing to its weight. Rifle companies sometimes carried one or two, but they were mostly relegated to firebase defense, supporting local security patrols and illumination at night.

The 81mm M29A1 mortar saw little use in the field owing to its weight. Rifle companies sometimes carried one or two, but they were mostly relegated to firebase defense, supporting local security patrols and illumination at night.

companies were A–D, and the CSC was usually designated Company E. Rifle platoons were numbered 1st–3rd, with the weapons or mortar platoon designated, e.g., Mortar Platoon, Company A. Rifle squads were designated 1st–3rd and the weapons squad as Weapons Squad, 1st Rifle Platoon. Fire teams were designated Alpha and Bravo.

Note that parenthesized functional and other descriptive designations followed the battalion/company designation and not the regimental designation because that described the battalion/company, not the regiment. Parenthesized designations, possibly two, could be spelled out or abbreviated. Common examples included: Airborne, or Abn; Airmobile, or Ambl; Mechanized, Mech or M; Combat, Cbt or C; Light, or Lt; Provisional, or Prov; Separate, or Sep. (which always followed any other parenthesized designation.) The abbreviations might be all in upper case.

Abbreviated unit designations are frequently rendered incorrectly, even in official documents. Company C, 1st Battalion (Mechanized), 47th Infantry would be abbreviated C/1-47 Inf (Mech) or (M) and Company C (Ranger), 75th Infantry as C-75 (Rgr). In this case, the parenthesized designation is after the full unit designation. One often sees C/1/47 Inf, but the second slash is incorrect. The slash indicates that the subordinate unit is organic to its parent unit. The hyphen only indicates that the battalion or separate company is tied by lineage to the "regiment."

The divisions

Army divisions were organized under the Reorganization Objective Army Division (ROAD, pronounced "ROW-ad"). The reorganization had begun in 1962 with the airborne divisions reorganized in 1964 and the first airmobile division created in 1965. There were five types of divisions: infantry, infantry (mechanized), armored, airborne, and airmobile. There were also similar separate brigades (with the exception of airmobile). The principles in the structure of the ROAD division were the recognition that no one standard division was capable of performing all missions, that divisions needed to be specialized to a degree, and that they required a flexible structure that could be tailored to meet the demands of different levels of conflict, terrain, climate, enemy capabilities, and other conditions. Organizational flexibility was the key. While optimally organized for conventional and nuclear warfare, the

ROAD divisions proved to be adaptable to Vietnam's counterinsurgency and low-level conventional environment.

Divisions had a common "division base" of command, combat support, and combat service support units. They were internally organized and equipped differently depending on the type of division, e.g., the mechanized and armored divisions' bases were virtually identical and the infantry divisions' very similar. The airborne division's base was similar to the infantry's as was the airmobile division's, but both were organized, equipped, and augmented with additional, specialized units to accommodate their means of transportation and delivery. The division base consisted of the division HHC, three brigade HHCs, division artillery (DIVARTY), division support command (DISCOM), and divisional troops.

The infantry division DIVARTY consisted of the HHB, DIVARTY, three 105mm howitzer battalions, and a 155mm/8in. howitzer battalion. The airborne and airmobile DIVARTYs lacked the general support battalion. The airmobile DIVARTY had an aerial rocket artillery battalion and an aviation artillery battery with observation helicopters.

The DISCOM of the infantry division had an HHC and band; maintenance, supply and transport, and medical battalions; and an administrative company. Airborne and airmobile divisions had a supply and service battalion rather than supply and transport. The airmobile division also had a transportation aircraft maintenance and supply battalion.

Divisional troops directly under the division HQ included the armored cavalry squadron; engineer combat, signal, and aviation battalions; and a military police company. Elements could be attached to the maneuver units. The division's three brigades possessed only an HHC. Eight to ten maneuver battalions (infantry, light infantry, airborne, airmobile, mechanized infantry, and tank) were assigned to the division and attached to the brigades as necessary, usually three or four. Additional maneuver battalions might be temporarily attached from another division, up to a total of 15. The numbers and types of battalions sometimes changed with additional battalions being added during a division's Vietnam service, and a few battalions converted from one type to another, mainly infantry to mechanized. Battalions could be switched between brigades, but they remained more or less attached to specific brigades throughout their service, although temporary attachment to other brigades was common. Airborne and airmobile divisions had a single type of infantry battalion, but some infantry divisions had one or two mechanized battalions and possibly a tank battalion. Usually a 105mm artillery battalion plus combat engineer, medical, and forward support (maintenance) companies were attached to support a brigade as the "forward support element."

There were also a number of habitual attachments to divisions: long-range patrol (LRP)/Ranger, military intelligence (MI), and Army Security Agency (ASA) companies; chemical[2], military history, and public information detachments plus combat tracker; and three scout dog platoons (one per brigade). Artillery, armored cavalry, aviation, and engineer units could be temporarily attached from other divisions or higher commands for specific operations. From 1967 divisions and brigades were required to form a one-to-two-week school session to train and acclimatize green troops bestowed with a catchy name.

Total strength figures are not provided for divisions and brigades as they varied so much, depending on the assigned numbers and types of maneuver battalions. USARV did attempt to maintain divisions at 102 percent of their authorized strength, but this was virtually impossible. In 1968 the actual strength of seven divisions ranged from 15,800–19,000 while separate brigades ran from 3,000–4,000.

---

2 Two chemical elements were normally assigned, one to assist the division chemical staff section in planning and coordination and the other to support chemical operations: flame and illumination devices emplaced at firebases, tear gas delivery systems, defoliation, flamethrower servicing, tunnel neutralization with tear gas blowers, etc.

Infantry division, TO&E 7E, 1966				
Unit			**Strength**	**TO&E**
HHC, Infantry Division			43-0-95	7-4E
HHC, Brigade (1st–3rd)			23-6-94	7-42E
Infantry Battalion (x9 or x8 & x1 mechanized infantry)[1]				
Division Artillery			169-15-1987	6-100E
	HHB, Division Artillery		34-4-167	6-302E
	Artillery Battalion (105mm towed) (x3)		36-3-448	6-155E
		HHSB	18-3-151	6-156E
		Artillery Battery (105mm towed) (Btry A–C)	6-0-99	6-157E
	Artillery Battalion (155mm towed, 8in. SP)		27-2-576	6-165E
		HHSB	15-2-155	6-166E
		Artillery Battery (155mm towed) (Btry A–C)	3-0-103	6-167E
		Artillery Battery (8in. SP) (Btry D)	3-0-106	6-358E
Division Support Command			141-23-1785	29-1E
	HHC & Band, Division Support Command		17-1-79	29-2E
	Quartermaster Supply & Motor Transportation Battalion		25-2-405	29-5E
		HHC	15-1-69	29-6E
		Quartermaster Supply & Service Company (Co A)	5-0-118	10-7E
		Transportation Motor Transport Company (Co B)	5-1-218	55-88E
	Ordnance Maintenance Battalion		29-14-648	29-15E
		HQ & Main Support Company (Co A)	15-4-260	9-16E
		Forward Support Company (Co A–C)	4-2-71	29-17E
		Transportation Aircraft Maintenance Company (Co D)	2-4-175	55-89E
	Medical Battalion		40-0-356	8-35E

Continues on following page

		HQ & Support Company	16-0-116	8-36E
		Medical Company (Co A–C)	8-0-80	8-37E
	Administrative Company		30-6-297	12-37E
Divisional Troops				
	Armored Cavalry Squadron		45-22-749	17-105E
		HHT	18-3-199	17-106E
		Armored Cavalry Troop (Trp A–C)	5-0-146	17-107E
		Air Cavalry Troop (Trp D)	12-19-112	17-108E
	Aviation Battalion		45-23-250	1-75E
		HHD	10-1-50	1-76E
		Assault Helicopter Company[2] (Co A)	13-16-87	1-77E
		Aviation General Support Company (Co B)	22-6-113	1-78E
	Engineer Battalion (Combat)		44-2-904	5-155E
		HHC	19-2-168	5-156E
		Engineer Company (Co A–C)	5-0-147	5-157E
	Signal Battalion		25-4-597	11-35E
		HHD	11-3-49	11-36E
		Command Operations Company (Co A)	4-1-189	11-37E
		Forward Communications Company (Co B)	5-0-167	11-38E
	Signal Support	Operations Company (Co C)	5-0-192	11-39E
	Military Police Company		9-1-179	19-27E
Typical Attachments				
	Airborne Infantry Ranger Company[3]		3-0-115	7-157E
	Military Intelligence Company (Division)[4]		66 total	30-17E
	ASA Company (Division Support)		118 total	32-57P
	Chemical Detachment &/or Platoon			
	Military History Detachment		1-0-1	20-17E
	Public Information Detachment (x2)			
	Infantry Platoon (Combat Tracker)		1-0-22	
	Infantry Platoon (Scout Dog) (x3, 1 per brigade)		1-0-27	7-167E

Notes:

Strength figures are listed as: Officers-Warrant Officers-Enlisted.

1 The number and types of maneuver battalions varied from 8–11. TO&Es are discussed separately.

2 Airmobile Company (Light) prior to July 1967.

3 Infantry Long-Range Patrol Company prior to February 1, 1969.

4 MI Detachment (Division) prior to December 26, 1967.

Infantry (TO&E 7E) and airborne (TO&E 57F) division, 1966

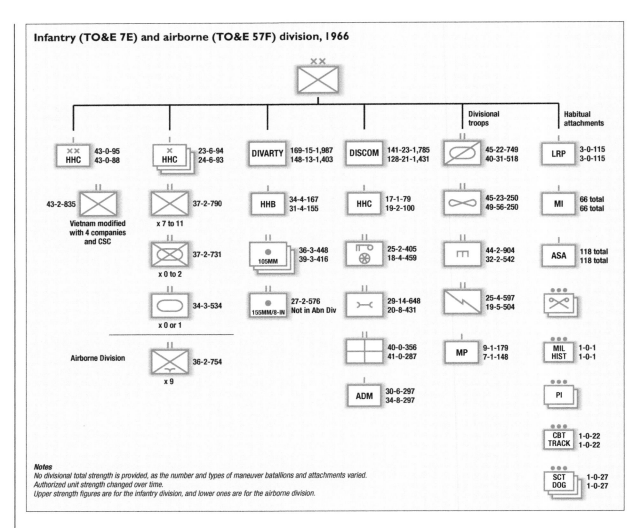

HHC	43-0-95 / 43-0-88
HHC	23-6-94 / 24-6-93
DIVARTY	169-15-1,987 / 148-13-1,403
DISCOM	141-23-1,785 / 128-21-1,431
Divisional troops	45-22-749 / 40-31-518
Habitual attachments — LRP	3-0-115 / 3-0-115

43-2-835 — **Vietnam modified with 4 companies and CSC**

37-2-790 (x 7 to 11)

37-2-731 (x 0 to 2)

34-3-534 (x 0 or 1)

Airborne Division — 36-2-754 (x 9)

HHB 34-4-167 / 31-4-155

105MM — 36-3-448 / 39-3-416

155MM/8-IN — 27-2-576 / Not in Abn Div

HHC 17-1-79 / 19-2-100

25-2-405 / 18-4-459

29-14-648 / 20-8-431

40-0-356 / 41-0-287

ADM 30-6-297 / 34-8-297

45-23-250 / 49-56-250

44-2-904 / 32-2-542

25-4-597 / 19-5-504

MP 9-1-179 / 7-1-148

MI 66 total / 66 total

ASA 118 total / 118 total

MIL HIST 1-0-1 / 1-0-1

PI

CBT TRACK 1-0-22 / 1-0-22

SCT DOG 1-0-27 / 1-0-27

Notes
No divisional total strength is provided, as the number and types of maneuver batallions and attachments varied.
Authorized unit strength changed over time.
Upper strength figures are for the infantry division, and lower ones are for the airborne division.

A rifle squad, just delivered by helicopter at a hilltop firebase, consolidates its position before its men dig in. Hilltop firebases were partly blasted clear by artillery, and then engineers cleared trees and debris to allow helicopters to deliver infantry and artillery.

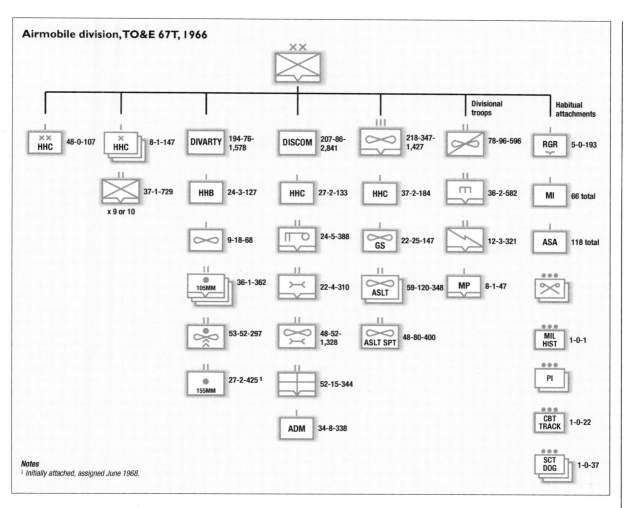

Airmobile division, TO&E 67T, 1966

Unit	Strength
HHC (×× div)	48-0-107
HHC (× bde)	8-1-147
(× bde)	37-1-729 x 9 or 10
DIVARTY	194-76-1,578
HHB	24-3-127
	9-18-68
105MM	36-1-362
	53-52-297
155MM	27-2-425 [1]
DISCOM	207-86-2,841
HHC	27-2-133
	24-5-388
	22-4-310
	48-52-1,328
	52-15-344
ADM	34-8-338
	218-347-1,427
HHC	37-2-184
GS	22-25-147
ASLT	59-120-348
ASLT SPT	48-80-400
	78-96-596
	36-2-582
	12-3-321
MP	8-1-47

Divisional troops

Habitual attachments

Unit	Strength
RGR	5-0-193
MI	66 total
ASA	118 total
MIL HIST	1-0-1
PI	
CBT TRACK	1-0-22
SCT DOG	1-0-37

Notes
[1] Initially attached, assigned June 1968.

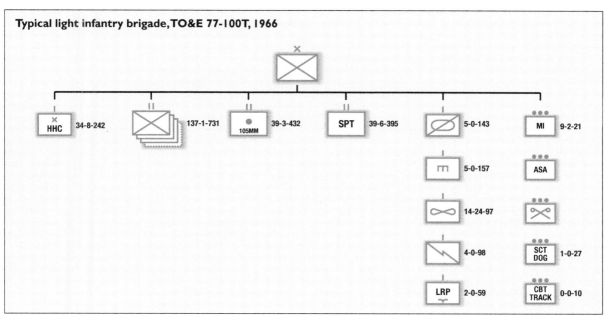

Typical light infantry brigade, TO&E 77-100T, 1966

Unit	Strength
HHC (× bde)	34-8-242
	137-1-731
105MM	39-3-432
SPT	39-6-395
	5-0-143
	5-0-157
	14-24-97
	4-0-98
LRP	2-0-59
MI	9-2-21
ASA	
SCT DOG	1-0-27
CBT TRACK	0-0-10

Brigade HHC, infantry division, TO&E 7-42E, 1966

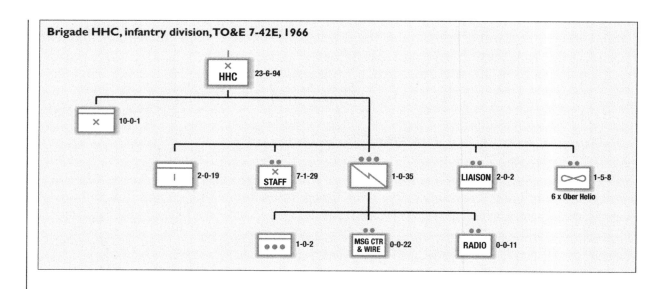

Airmobile division, TO&E 67T, 1966

Unit				Strength	TO&E
HHC, Airmobile Division				48-0-107	67-2T
HHC, Brigade (1st–3rd)				25-17-171	67-42T
Infantry Battalion (Airmobile) (x8–10)[1]				37-1-729	7-55T
Division Artillery				194-76-1578	6-700T
	HHB, Division Artillery			24-3-127	6-701T
	Aviation Artillery Battery			9-18-68	6-702T
	Artillery Battalion (105mm towed) (Ambl) (x3)			36-1-362	6-705T
		HHSB		18-1-113	6-706T
		Artillery Battery (105mm towed) (Btry A–C)		6-0-83	6-707T
	Artillery Battalion (155mm towed)[2]			27-2-425	6-425E
		HHSB		18-2-216	6-426E
		Artillery Battery (155mm towed) (Btry A–C)		3-0-103	6-437E
	Artillery Battalion (Aerial Rocket)			53-52-297	6-725T
		HHSB		44-4-69	6-726T
		Artillery Battery (Aerial Rocket) (Btry A–C)		13-16-76	6-727T
Aviation Group				218-347-1427	1-100T
	HHC, Aviation Group			37-2-184	1-101T
	General Support Aviation Company			22-25-147	1-102T

Continues on following page

	Assault Helicopter Battalion (x2)		59-120-348	1-155T
		HHC	13-2-80	1-156T
		Assault Helicopter Company (Co A–C)	10-35-68	1-158T
		Aerial Weapons Company (Co D)	16-64-13	1-157T
	Assault Support Helicopter Battalion		41-80-400	1-165T
		HHC	14-2-73	1-166T
		Assault Support Helicopter Company (Co A–C)	9-26-109	1-167T
Division Support Command			207-86-2841	29-41T
	HHC & Band, Division Support Command		27-2-133	29-42T
	Quartermaster Supply Battalion		24-5-388	29-95T
		HHSC	16-3-121	29-96T
		Quartermaster Supply Company	7-1-288	29-97T
		Quartermaster Aerial Support Equipment Det (Abn)	1-1-39	29-98T
	Ordnance Maintenance Battalion		22-4-310	29-85T
		HQ & Main Support Company	13-4-190	20-86T
		Forward Support Detachment (Det A–C)	3-0-40	29-87T
	Transportation Aircraft Maintenance Battalion		48-52-1328	55-405T
		HHC	12-4-88	55-406T
		Transportation Aircraft Maint & Supply Co (Co A–D)	9-12-310	55-407T
	Medical Battalion		52-15-344	8-25T
		HQ & Support Company	27-15-146	8-26T
		Medical Company (Co A–C)	8-0-66	8-27T
	Administrative Company		34-8-338	12-77T
Divisional Troops				
	Air Cavalry Squadron		78-96-596	17-95T
		HHT	19-6-157	17-96T
		Air Cavalry Troop (Trp A–C)	18-30-104	17-98T
		Cavalry Troop (Trp D)	5-0-127	17-99T
	Engineer Battalion (Combat)		36-2-582	5-215T
		HHC	21-2246	5-216T
		Engineer Company (Co A–C)	5-0-112	5-217T
	Signal Battalion		12-3-321	11-205T

Continues on following page

HHSC		6-2-68	11-206T
	Command Operations Company	6-1-253	11-207T
Military Police Company		8-1-147	19-87T

Notes:
Strength figures are listed as: Officers-Warrant Officers-Enlisted.
Typical attachments were for an infantry division plus additional small aviation units.
1 When initially deployed, three of the 1st CavDiv's airmobile battalions, a 105mm battalion, 1st Bde HHC, an engineer company, a
   medical company, and forward support detachment were airborne qualified. They had the same TO&Es as their nonairborne counterparts.
2 Initially attached but assigned June 1968.

The concept of the airmobile division saw it with almost 500 aircraft but only about one-third of the ground vehicles of an infantry division. One-third of its combat elements could be airlifted in one move by organic helicopters. It was not just tactical mobility though; all aspects of the division's operations would be enhanced by aviation: reconnaissance, fire support, logistics, command and control, among others. It would be ideal in Vietnam to employ an airmobile division in larger areas of operation over difficult terrain. Its flexibility and ability to quickly introduce large forces into remote areas kept the enemy off balance. The air cavalrymen could arrive at any time from any direction with little or no warning. The division was also able to quickly dispatch aerial fire support, introduce reinforcements, reposition units in blocking positions or to pursue the enemy, resupply engaged forces, evacuate casualties, and extract forces in unfavorable positions. Its aerial reconnaissance and target acquisition capabilities were extensive.

Separate brigades

A separate combined arms brigade was self-contained with organic support elements. It provided an agile unit to serve as a reaction force or as a "fire brigade" to be deployed where necessary. It was also assigned its own tactical area of responsibility like a division, albeit smaller. Sometimes it would be attached to a division for a specific operation.

A separate infantry brigade had a brigade HHC, three or four maneuver battalions, 105mm artillery battalion, support battalion, armored cavalry troop, and engineer company. Often attached were a signal company, long-range patrol detachment/Ranger company; various detachments (chemical,

A Bell UH-1H Iroquois utility helicopter offloads infantrymen. Better known as the Huey or "slick," the Iroquois was the workhorse of the war.

military intelligence, military history, public information, combat tracker); and a scout dog platoon. It was found that a fourth battalion greatly enhanced its capabilities by allowing one battalion to rest and provide security while keeping three actively employed.

Typical separate light infantry brigade, TO&E 77-100T, 1966		
Unit	**Strength**	**TO&E**
HHC, Infantry Brigade	34-8-242	77-102T
Infantry Battalions (Light) (x4)	37-1-731	7-175T
Field Artillery Battalion (105mm towed)	39-3-432	6-115T
HHSB	18-3-135	6-116T
Artillery Battery (105mm towed) (Btry A–C) 7-0-99		6-117T
Support Battalion	39-6-395	29-245T
HHD	12-0-50	29-246T
Administrative Company (Co A)	9-2-95	12-197T
Medical Company (Co B)	8-0-72	8-197T
Maintenance & Supply Company (Co C)	9-4-179	29-247T
Armored Cavalry Troop	5-0-143	17-117T
Engineer Combat Company	5-0-157	5-107T
Typical Attachments		
Signal Company	4-0-98	
Aviation Company	14-24-97	1-47E
Airborne Infantry Ranger Company[1]	2-0-59	7-157E
Military Intelligence Detachment (Brigade)	9-2-21	30-14E
ASA Detachment (Radio Research)		
Chemical Detachment	1-0-4	
Military History Detachment	1-0-1	20-17E
Public Information Detachment	1-0-4	
Infantry Platoon (Scout Dog)	1-0-27	7-167E
Infantry Detachment (Combat Tracker)	0-0-10	

Note:
Strength figures are listed as: Officers-Warrant Officers-Enlisted.
1 Infantry Long-Range Patrol Detachment prior to February 1, 1969.

The Boeing CH-47A Chinook medium cargo helicopter, better known as the "Forty-Seven" or "shithook." It could deliver light vehicles, ammunition, supplies, and an understrength platoon. It often brought in follow-on troops once Huey-delivered infantry had secured the LZ.

The separate airborne brigade (TO&E 57-100F) was similarly organized, but its support battalion had administrative, medical, supply and service, and maintenance companies, which was different to other separate brigades.

When divisional brigades were detached from their parent division they received a "slice" of support elements and were organized similarly to a separate brigade. A provisional support battalion would be formed for logistical, maintenance, medical, and administrative support.

It can be said that 12 separate brigades served in Vietnam. The 1st Bde, 101st AbnDiv deployed 2$\frac{1}{2}$ years before its parent division. The 11th, 196th, and 198th Infantry Brigades (Light) were consolidated into the AMERICAL (the name meaning American New Caledonia, in 1942) Division. The 199th remained separate as did the 173rd AbnBde, and the 196th again served as a separate brigade after the AMERICAL Division stood down. The 1st Bde, 5th InfDiv (Mech) and 3rd Bde, 82nd AbnDiv deployed to Vietnam augmented as separate brigades while their parent divisions remained in the States. Three other divisional brigades (1st Bde, 1st CavDiv; 3rd Bde, 9th InfDiv; 2nd Bde, 25th InfDiv) remained in Vietnam for varying time frames after their parent divisions departed and were augmented to operate as separate brigades. The 11th ACR also operated as a separate brigade.

Air mobility allowed for standby reaction forces to be delivered on the battlefield, giving commanders the ability to respond rapidly to changing situations and to influence combat power at unprecedented speed.

Maneuver battalions

Divisions and brigades existed to support maneuver battalions, the real fighters. Most of these battalions were infantry, but three tank battalions served in Vietnam.

Maneuver battalions			
Battalion		**Strength**	**TO&E**
Infantry Battalion		37-2-790	7-15E
	HHC	19-2-268	7-16E
	Rifle Company (x3)	6-0-174	7-18E
Infantry Battalion (Airborne)		36-2-754	7-35E
	HHC	18-2-232	7-36E
	Rifle Company (x3)	6-0-174	7-37E
Infantry Battalion (Airmobile)		37-1-729	7-55T
	HHC	14-1-119	7-56T
	Rifle Company (x3)	6-0-164	7-57T
	CSC	5-0-118	7-58T
Infantry Battalion (Light)		37-1-731	7-175T
	HHC	14-1-121	7-176T
	Rifle Company (x3)	6-0-164	7-177T
	CSC	5-0-118	7-187T
Infantry Battalion (Light)[1]		43-2-835	7-175T
	HHC	15-2-147	7-176T
	Rifle Company (x4)	6-0-158	7-177T
	CSC	4-0-96	7-187T
Infantry Battalion (Mechanized)		37-2-860	7-45E
	HHC	19-2-281	7-46E
	Rifle Company (x3)	6-0-193	7-47E
Tank Battalion		34-3-534	17-35E
	HHC	19-3-279	17-36E
	Tank Company (x3)	5-0-85	17-37E

Notes:
Strength figures are listed as: Officers-Warrant Officers-Enlisted.
1 In late 1967, infantry, airborne, and airmobile battalions received a fourth rifle company and a CSC. Mechanized battalions did not. Later TO&Es had slightly different strengths.

Regardless of type, infantry battalions were of a basic common organization. The battalion HQ consisted of the CO, XO, staff officers, and sergeant major. The headquarters company was organized into a company HQ, battalion HQ section with staff assistants and specialists, and several platoons:

Communications platoon – Operated the message center, laid telephone wire, and repaired radios.
Support platoon – Transportation section with cargo and fuel trucks, supply section for supplies and ammunition distribution, and four to six company mess teams. (Support platoons were called service platoons in airmobile and light infantry battalions.)

Headquarters and headquarters company, infantry battalion, TO&E 7-16E, 1966

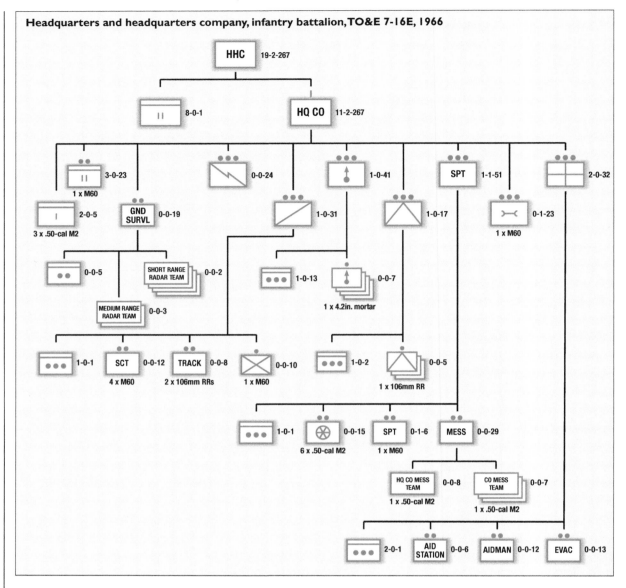

Maintenance platoon – Performed vehicle maintenance and recovery.
Medical platoon – Aid station section operated the aid station, evacuation section operated frontline jeep ambulances, and aidman section provided medics to the companies, invariably nicknamed "Doc."

The headquarters company might also contain several combat platoons. In airmobile and light infantry battalions these platoons were assigned to the combat support company.

Scout platoon – Conducted reconnaissance, screening, and security missions. (Called a reconnaissance platoon in infantry, airborne, airmobile, and light infantry, and called a scout platoon in mechanized and tank battalions, in Vietnam they were generally all called scout platoons.)
Antitank platoon – Operated jeep-mounted 106mm recoilless rifles (not in tank battalion).

Rifle company, infantry battalion, TO&E 7-18E, 1966

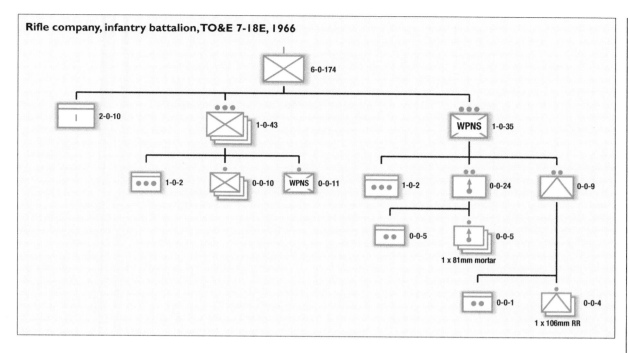

Heavy Mortar platoon – Operated 4.2in. mortars (81mm in airmobile and light battalions).

Ground Surveillance Section – Operated four AN/PPS-4 and two AN/TPS-33 radars (mechanized battalions only).

The HHC of the mechanized battalions and tank battalions had a number of tracked vehicles in support roles, and the maintenance platoon was larger than that of other battalions. The mech battalion's TO&E showed that two M132A1 mechanized flamethrowers were assigned to the supply section, although crews were not provided. They were to be manned by scratch crews, if needed, but most units formed a platoon of four Zippos.

The CSC freed the headquarters company CO from having to control and support combat elements, allowing him to concentrate on service support and

An M48A3 Patton tank covers a route security patrol with its 90mm guns and machine guns. Armor was originally thought to be of little use in Vietnam, but it proved its value in route security and sweeps.

administration. Most of these combat support assets were unneeded, had a reduced need, or were re-equipped and their roles were modified. Airmobile, light infantry, and tank battalions did not have ground surveillance radar sections.

The scout platoons were organized and equipped differently, depending on the type of battalion, but normally had a scout section with four machine-gun jeeps, an antitank section with two jeep-mounted 106mm recoilless rifles, an 81mm mortar squad, and a rifle squad. The last two were carried by 3/4-ton trucks. The vehicles were reassigned to other duties and the platoons reorganized into three squads of foot-mobile scouts, little different from a rifle platoon. They were sometimes given colorful nicknames or called LRPs (long-range patrol units, pronounced "LURP" but should never be spelled as such), which they really were not. The airmobile and light infantry reconnaissance platoons had only three ten-man dismounted scout squads. Mechanized and tank battalion scout platoons had only two scout sections with nine M113A1 armored personnel carriers (APCs) rather than M114A1 reconnaissance vehicles. Some mechanized rifle companies added a 10–12-man dismounted reconnaissance team or squad.

Antitank platoons were mostly disbanded, although a few guns may have been kept for base defense, but this was seldom. The same applied to the mortar platoon, although the 4.2in. mortar may have been replaced by the 81mm, which was already organic to airmobile and light infantry battalion mortar platoons. Often HHC personnel from the antitank and mortar platoons and ground surveillance section were formed into a Company D along with personnel from the rifle company weapons platoons. Some incorporated their reconnaissance platoon into the company as a rifle platoon. Those battalions possessing a CSC often used it for the new Company D, and the remaining reconnaissance and mortar platoons were reassigned to the HHC. D companies formed in-country, or "out of hide," were usually understrength compared with the others and were mainly used for firebase security. Some mech battalions also formed a Company D from HHC antitank and scout platoons, company antitank sections, and replacements.

Even within the same division, battalions reorganized their assets differently. When the 1st CavDiv deployed to Vietnam, most of its battalions reorganized their 106mm RR (recoilless rifle)-armed antitank platoons as machine-gun platoons with M60s and reassigned the weapons carriers to other duties. This allowed the crews to reinforce firepower with a usable weapon. One battalion, however, the 2-7th Cavalry, simply armed the crews with M16 rifles, and each man carried two or three light antitank weapons (LAWs), which added little to unit firepower. These platoons disappeared as manpower dwindled.

Rifle companies had a headquarters, three rifle platoons, and a weapons platoon. A mortar platoon was present in the case of airmobile and light infantry battalions. Regardless of type, the company headquarters were similarly manned. All personnel were armed with rifles except the CO who was armed with a pistol, although, in reality he acquired a rifle. The armorer or clerk had an M79 and a pistol. Wiremen, switchboard operators, and radio mechanics were often concentrated in the HHC. In the field about the only personnel comprising the company headquarters were the CO, the XO or first sergeant (one remained with the company rear), and a couple of radio-telephone operators (RTOs). Some companies employed an SFC or SSG "field first sergeant" to allow the first sergeant to run the company rear. The "company rear" remained in a firebase, handling administration and supplies.

The standard rifle company headquarters had a 2 1/2-ton cargo truck with trailer and a jeep with trailer. The airborne company headquarters had a 1/2-ton cargo carrier and a jeep and trailer, while the airmobile company had only a 1/2-ton cargo carrier, and the light infantry had a jeep without trailer. All these vehicles remained in the rear and were taken up by the battalion, along with recoilless rifle jeeps and weapons/mortar platoon vehicles.

Rifle company headquarters

Duty Position	Rank	Inf	Abn	Ambl	Light	Mech[1]
Company CO	CPT	1	1	1	1	1
Company XO	1LT	1	1	1	1	1
First Sergeant	1SG	1	1	1	1	1
Supply Sergeant	SSG	1	1	1	1	1
Communications Chief	SGT	1	1	1	1	1
Armorer	SP4	1	1	1	1	--
Company Clerk	SP4	1	1	1	1	1
Field Switchboard Operator	SP4	1	--	1	1	--
Radio Mechanic	SP4	1	--	1	--	--
Radio-Telephone Operator	PFC	2	2	2	2	1
Wireman	PFC	2	2 [2]	--	--	--
Supply Clerk	PFC	--	1	--	--	--
Messenger	PFC	--	1	--	--	--
Personnel Carrier Driver	PFC	--	--	--	--	2
Total		13	13	11	10	9

Notes:

1 The mech company HQ also possessed a 13-man maintenance section with motor sergeant (SSG), 5x tracked vehicle mechanics (1x SP5, 4x SP4), 2x mechanic helpers (PFC), 2x recovery mechanics (1x SP5, 1x SP4), 2x radio mechanics (1x SP5, 1x SP4), and an armorer (SP4).

2 Also field switchboard operators.

The mechanized company headquarters had two M113A1s, one for the CO and the other a mobile rear command post (CP) for the XO, a 2 1/2-ton truck with trailer, and a jeep and trailer. The maintenance section had an M113A1, an M578 light recovery vehicle, and a 3/4-ton truck with trailer.

Regardless of the type of company, rifle platoons were similarly armed and organized with 44 men. The platoon headquarters had a platoon commander (almost always called a "platoon leader"), a platoon sergeant, and an RTO. The three ten-man rifle squads consisted of a squad leader and two fire teams (Alpha and Bravo) with a team leader, an automatic rifleman, and a grenadier. One team had two riflemen and the other had one. The 11-man weapons squad had a leader, two machine gunners and assistants, two antitank gunners and assistants, and two ammunition bearers.

The 47-man mechanized rifle platoon was organized somewhat differently. Each of the four squads possessed an M113A1 APC mounting a .50cal machine gun. The three-man headquarters split up to ride in squad carriers. The rifle squads had an extra man as a carrier driver, and one of the weapons squad's ammunition bearers doubled as a driver.

All rifle squad members were armed with rifles except the grenadiers who had a 40mm M79 and pistol. Antitank and machine gunners and assistants carried pistols while the weapons squad leader and ammunition bearers had rifles. There were two M60 machine guns and two 90mm M67 recoilless rifles. The light infantry weapons squad had two 3½in. bazookas instead of 90mm recoilless rifles. Mechanized rifle squads had an extra M60 that could be carried by a rifleman, or more commonly mounted at the cargo hatch. On paper the airmobile and light platoons had one M9-7 flamethrower, and the standard rifle company headquarters had three. Other companies lacked them, but they were simply not used in Vietnam.

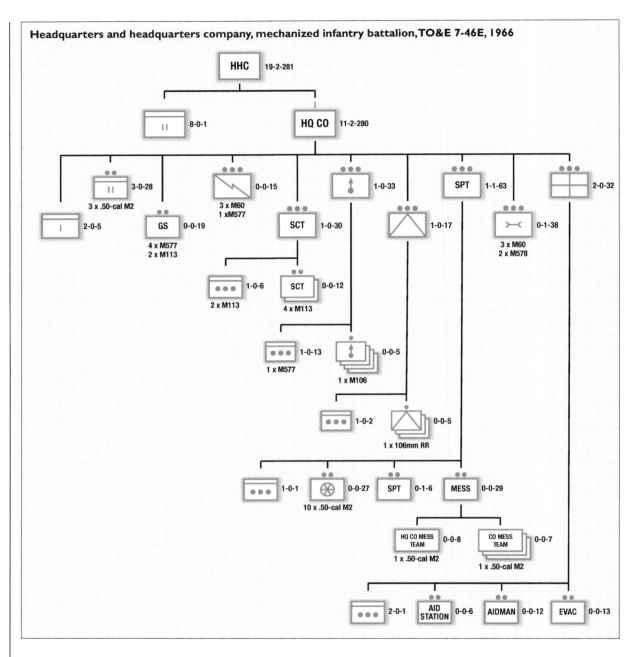

Headquarters and headquarters company, mechanized infantry battalion, TO&E 7-46E, 1966

The preceding accords with the TO&Es. However, the reality was very different and bore little resemblance to published TO&Es. When units first deployed to Vietnam, they were organized and armed according to the TO&E, but with combat losses, illness, personnel detailed to firebase duties and on R&R, and slow replacement flow, platoon strength declined. The employment of weapons changed greatly. It was seldom that the 90mm RRs or even the lighter 3.5in. bazookas were carried to the field, and instead they were placed in storage. There were instances in which one per platoon or even just one in the company might be carried. Their crews became riflemen. In 1967 one 90mm and crew were withdrawn from the TO&E, but the remaining RR was used very little. With the issue of the M16A1 rifle, there were no longer any squad automatic riflemen. Ostensibly they were "authorized" to fire full-

Rifle company, mechanized infantry battalion, TO&E 7-47E, 1966

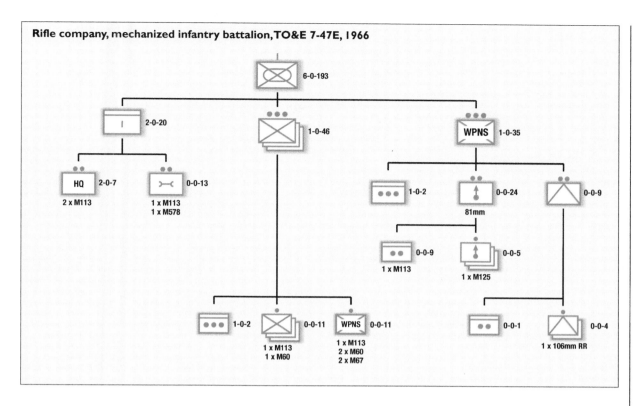

Tank company, tank battalion, TO&E 17-37E, 1966

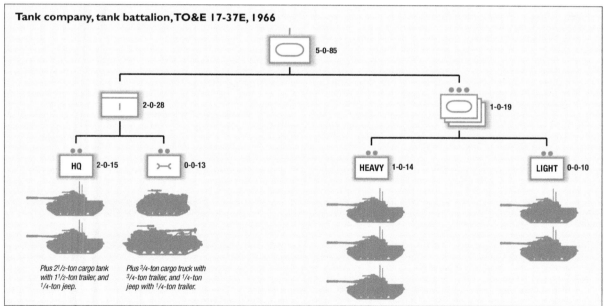

Plus 2¹/₂-ton cargo tank with 1¹/₂-ton trailer, and ¹/₄-ton jeep.

Plus ³/₄-ton cargo truck with ³/₄-ton trailer, and ¹/₄-ton jeep with ¹/₄-ton trailer.

automatic and were provided an inadequate clip-on bipod. In reality they became riflemen as did the antitank gunners, their assistants, and both ammunition bearers. Assistant machine gunners also drew rifles.

As platoon strength dwindled even further, it was aggravated by the lack of NCOs. There were 11 NCOs in a rifle platoon, and by 1967 often fewer than 50 percent were available. NCOs were being lost in combat and others were leaving the service or retiring, while senior NCOs who remained were being promoted to

The "track"

The M113 armored personnel carrier was adopted in 1963, followed by the M113A1 in 1964, which saw the widest use in Vietnam. Essentially an aluminum armored box on a full-tracked chassis, the "one-one-three" was a "battle taxi" armed with a .50cal. M2 machine gun on the commander's cupola and carrying 12 troops including the "track commander" (TC) and driver. The armored cavalry assault vehicle (ACAV, pronounced "A-cav") added a shield and tub around the .50cal. and a 7.62mm M60 machine gun with shield on either side of the top cargo hatch. It was not uncommon for additional machine guns, recoilless rifles, and automatic grenade launchers to be retrofitted. Troop egress was accomplished through a rear drop ramp, in which an individual troop door was set. The aluminum armor protected from small arms and shell fragments, but it could be defeated by RPGs, recoilless rifles, and 12.7mm machine guns. Mines were a real threat. The floor was provided with two layers of sandbags and further covered with ration and ammunition boxes. The troops rode exposed on top, a safer alternative. The 212hp diesel engine gave it a maximum road speed of 40 mph and a cruising range of 300 mi. The M113 gave reasonably good cross-country mobility, but its low ground clearance could cause it to bog down in deep mud or "belly-up" on stumps and fallen trees. It was amphibious with minimal preparation, making it useful for crossing rivers and canals. The M113 chassis provided the basis for the 4.2in. M106A1 mortar carrier, 81mm M125A1 mortar carrier, M132A1 "Zippo" mechanized flamethrower, 20mm Vulcan XM741 SP air defense vehicle, M577A1 "high hat" command post vehicle (also used as aid stations and fire direction centers), 6-ton M548 cargo carrier, XM45E1 flamethrower servicing vehicle, and the smaller M114A1 armored reconnaissance vehicle. (See Osprey Vanguard 34, *The M113 Series*.)

out-of-platoon positions. The vast majority of enlisted men were leaving the Army after their two- or three-year enlistment, reducing the number of potential NCOs. Additionally, once a soldier completed a Vietnam tour, he could not be returned for 25 months, unless volunteering.

The way platoons really looked on the ground bore little resemblance to TO&Es. Platoon strength was typically 20–30 men organized into two or three squads. The fire team concept was often abandoned, and in such cases even assistant squad leaders were not designated. The weapons squad usually ceased to exist. The two M60s were either assigned directly to rifle squads, sometimes with a third added, or to the platoon headquarters. Often assistant machine gunners used rifles, and gunners did not bother with pistols. Rifle squads often had only five to eight men. Squad leaders were typically sergeants or SP4s, while fire team leaders, if employed, were SP4s or PFCs. Other platoons retained four squads, three five-to-six-man rifle squads, and a seven-man weapons squad with two M60s. Some platoons fielded only two six-to-eight-man rifle squads, but a full 11-man weapons squad had two M60s – each with a gunner, an assistant, and three ammunition bearers who also supplied suppressive rifle fire carrying 1,500 rounds. It was not uncommon for only two squads of 9–12 men with an organic two-man machine gun crew to be organized in order to provide a higher strength. Some squads organized into a "point team" with a point man (M16 on full-auto or shotgun), grenadier, and two riflemen, and a "gun team" with an M60 gunner and an assistant, four or five riflemen, plus the squad leader. Two grenadiers were usually retained, but some small squads had only one in order not to reduce rifle strength. Some grenadiers carried an M16A1 instead of a pistol, and many carried only an M79 because their secondary weapon was easily lost. Often, when only two squads were employed, and because of the inexperience of some squad leaders, the platoon leader and platoon sergeant would each take charge of a squad when engaged. Medics became a fixture in the platoon headquarters, and, if 81mm mortars were taken to the field, a mortar observer, with or without his own RTO, would accompany the platoon. In some units there was an RTO with an extra radio for the platoon sergeant.

On occasion some platoons concentrated their grenadiers in a temporary grouping for fire support. They might do the same with a number of riflemen carrying multiple LAWs. In both instances the grouped weapons would be used against bunkers or snipers. One or two Kit Carson scouts[3] were often attached to platoons. These were former VC/NVA – *hoi chanhs* (returnees) who had *chieu hoied* (defected, or rallied). After undertaking a two-week course, they proved a valuable asset for detecting enemy activity and signs, booby traps, and edifying US troops on tactics and techniques. From September 1967 a minimum of 100 Kit Carsons were authorized per division.

There were times late in the war when platoons were brought up to near full strength. This was from early 1970 through early 1972 when the US troop withdrawal was in full swing. Personnel with less than seven months remaining on their tour were transferred from departing battalions to others.

---

3 Called "Tiger Scouts" in the 9th InfDiv.

Company COs found themselves with nearly full platoons, although NCO shortages persisted, even with young soldiers being rushed through "Shake 'n Bake" NCO Candidate Courses. Strength would soon begin to decline with casualties and rotations home, an endless cycle.

Mechanized platoons changed too. Often only three or just two APCs were operational, so troops would load on whatever was running. Whereas the conventional mechanized platoon was organized as other platoons and capable of fighting dismounted, in Vietnam the squads essentially became "track crews" of five to seven men. They fought from their "track" dismounting only to provide security and for short-distance "cloverleaf" sweeps.

Company weapons and mortar platoons mostly disappeared. The mortars and recoilless rifles were not needed. Some companies retained one or two mortars for use in firebases and others might replace the battalion 4.2in. mortars. Occasionally one or two mortars might be carried to the field. Some weapons platoons with two mortars maintained a 20–30-plus strength enabling up to 60 rounds to be carried. The antitank section was sometimes retained strictly as mortar ammunitions bearers, carrying three 9 lb rounds each. Other companies maintained a 12–15-man mortar "platoon" with only one 81mm, which may or may not have been taken to the field. If the mortars were not carried, some of the platoon might serve as riflemen. In dense forests there was no overhead clearance to fire them. In some instances one or more mortars might be helicoptered in to defend a night location or temporary firebase. Often they were used only for illumination with artillery defensive fires being relied on.

The 5.56mm M16A1 rifle was the principal shoulder weapon. The "black rifle" had its teething problems, but, once most defects were corrected, it proved to be a suitable, if not perfect, weapon.

The 36-man mechanized weapons platoons were more or less retained. The three-man platoon headquarters had a jeep and trailer. The mortar section had a nine-man headquarters with an M113A1 and a 1½ -ton cargo trailer for the fire direction center. There were three squads, each with an 81mm M125A1 mortar carrier. Their crews would fight from them much like rifle platoon tracks. The antitank section had a one-man headquarters and two squads, each with a jeep-mounted 106mm RR. These may have been deleted, or the rifles may have been mounted on rifle platoon APCs.

Recognizing, in 1966, the value of a fourth rifle company and a CSC, US Army, Pacific published General Order 149 on September 10, 1967. This order authorized these companies for all infantry battalions except mechanized and the 9th InfDiv's. All other infantry, airborne, and airmobile battalions were reorganized as modified light infantry battalions. Apparently not all battalions organized a CSC. The 9th InfDiv was not authorized fourth companies until late 1968, although some battalions managed to form provisional D Companies. The three-company battalion was effective in conventional linear operations, but in Vietnam more flexibility was needed. Four companies allowed one to be used for firebase defense or as a reserve or reaction force – it could not provide both security and be on standby to depart the base.

The increase of combat power achieved by adding a fourth company can be demonstrated by the experience of the 9th InDiv. In early 1968 it fielded 21 rifle and six mechanized companies for a total of 27. In late 1968 its six infantry battalions had 28 companies when fourth companies were added, and

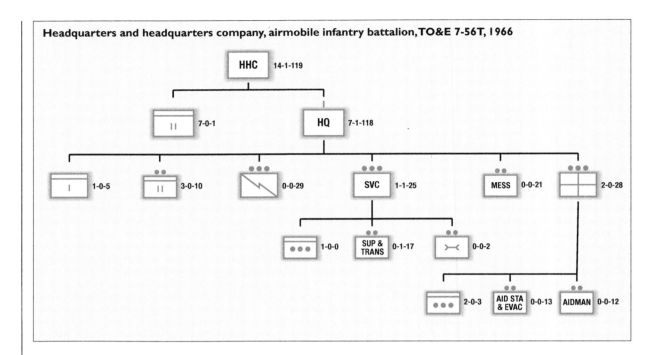

Headquarters and headquarters company, airmobile infantry battalion, TO&E 7-56T, 1966

Rifle company, airmobile infantry battalion, TO&E 7-57T, 1966

there remained six mech companies. There were now 34 companies altogether, a 25.9 percent increase. An additional infantry battalion was added in April 1968, giving the division 32 rifle and six mech companies to total 38 companies, a 40.7 percent increase over the original structure. With a mech battalion converted to straight leg in September 1968, the division now had 36 rifle and three mech for 39 companies, 12 more than it did when it deployed, a 44.4 percent increase. This created enough companies to form four battalions but without the need for additional headquarters and combat support company overhead.

What were known as "Company D Packets" were raised in the States from recruits, officers, and NCOs drawn from stateside units plus recent OCS and Noncommissioned Officer Candidate School (NCOCS) graduates. They were given minimal training and deployed in August and September 1967. Most if not all battalion commanders broke them up among the existing companies and created a new Company D, with a quarter of the green troops filled out with veterans from the other companies. From late 1967 units deploying from

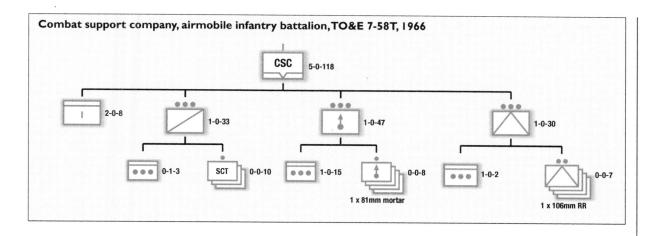

Combat support company, airmobile infantry battalion, TO&E 7-58T, 1966

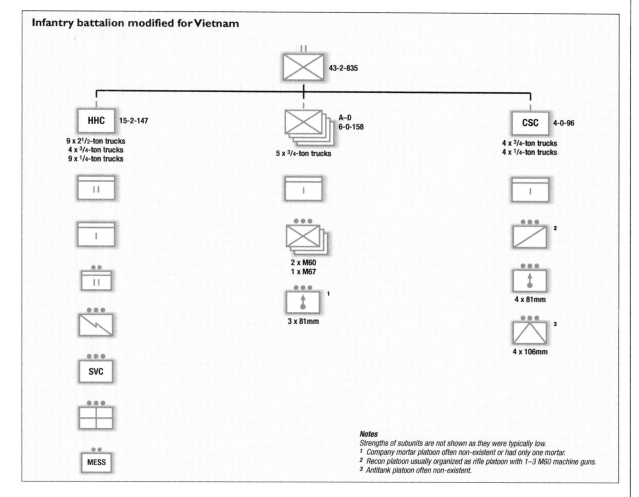

Infantry battalion modified for Vietnam

Notes
Strengths of subunits are not shown as they were typically low.
1 *Company mortar platoon often non-existent or had only one mortar.*
2 *Recon platoon usually organized as rifle platoon with 1–3 M60 machine guns.*
3 *Antitank platoon often non-existent.*

the States organized fourth companies. This measure was only used in Vietnam and disappeared after the war.

Three tank battalions (TO&E 17-35) served in Vietnam with the 4th and 25th InfDiv and the 1st Bde, 5th InfDiv. The HHC was similar to that of a mechanized battalion's with the addition of a headquarters tank section (3xM48A3) and an armored vehicle-launched bridge section (2xAVLB). Like the mechanized battalion, tank battalion support elements possessed a large number of full-tracked support vehicles.[4] In Vietnam the HHCs were split into separate headquarters and service companies (Company D), the latter with the support and maintenance platoons, AVLB section, and possibly all or part of the three company maintenance sections.

The tank companies had a headquarters with a headquarters section of two officers and 15 enlisted plus a 13-man maintenance section similar to the mech rifle company's. The three tank platoons had five tanks crewed by four men. No. 1 tank was commanded by the platoon leader, and No. 4 was commanded by the platoon sergeant. The gunners in these two tanks were designated assistant tank commanders (TCs) and rated sergeants. In the other three tanks, the gunners were SP5s. All five drivers were SP5s and the loaders were PFCs. Tank platoons operated as two sections; No. 1–3 tanks under the platoon leader and No. 4 and No. 5 under the platoon sergeant. Tank crewmen each had a .45cal pistol, and two .45cal M3A1 submachine guns ("grease guns") were stowed in the tank. The two tanks in the company headquarters section were commanded by SSG tank commanders. The CO and XO could replace the TC. The headquarters had two jeeps and a 2½-ton truck with trailer. The maintenance section had an M88 armored recovery vehicle, an M113A1, a jeep and trailer, and a ¾-ton truck and trailer.

A single airborne tank company served with the 173rd AbnBde from 1965–69. Company D (Tank) (Airborne), 16th Armor was initially equipped with 15 90mm M56 Scorpion SP AT (self-propelled antitank) guns. It turned in nine and received 11 M113 APCs and four 4.2in. M106 mortar carriers. It deployed to Vietnam with one platoon of six "SPATs," two platoons of five APCs, the mortar platoon, and one APC in the headquarters. In Vietnam it received an M577 CP (command post) vehicle and an M113 for the mortar fire direction control center. The SPAT had an open mounting and lacked armor, making the crew extremely vulnerable. In mid-1966 the SPATs were withdrawn, and five more APCs were added. The APCs were converted to armored cavalry assault vehicles (ACAVs) with one per platoon mounting a 90mm RR. The unit was actually authorized Sheridans, but the ACAVs offered more utility carrying attached infantrymen.

Armored cavalry

Several types of armored cavalry units were employed in Vietnam. Infantry divisions had the same type of armored cavalry squadron as armored and mechanized divisions. There were five of these to include two detached from stateside armored divisions. Armored cav units were multi-purpose and tasked with a wide range of conventional missions. Their training was broader based and more complex than any other, being organized as combined arms units down to platoon level and even possessing their own aviation capability. Besides performing aggressive reconnaissance, they conducted covering, flank and gap screening, and served in rear area security missions and as a division reserve. When necessary they could fight as mounted infantry. In Vietnam they conducted offensive operations, kept lines of communication open, and secured base areas, making good use of their armored mobile firepower and organic aviation.

The squadron HHT consisted of the troop headquarters, squadron headquarters section, ground surveillance radar section and communications, support, maintenance, medical, and flamethrower (4xM132A1) platoons. The armored cavalry troop (called "ground cav troops") had a headquarters with headquarters, ground surveillance, and maintenance sections.

In Vietnam, the 38-man armored cavalry platoon had nine vehicles:

---

4 See Osprey *Vietnam Tracks: Armor in Battle 1945–75* (Revised Edition).

Platoon HQ – 1x M113A1 ACAVs, 2x men.
Scout section – 4x M113A1 ACAVs, 12x men.
Tank section – 2x M48A3 tanks, 8x men.
Rifle squad – 1x M113A1 APC/ACAV, 11x men.
Support squad – 1x 4.2in M106A1 mortar carrier, 5x men.

In Vietnam the M48A3 tanks or additional ACAVs replaced the standard M41A3 Walker Bulldog light tanks. From 1969 Sheridan tanks were used by some units. The main scout vehicle was supposed to be the M114A1 armored reconnaissance vehicle, but M113A1 ACAVs were used instead. Forty M114s had earlier been issued to ARVN units, but the vehicles were soon withdrawn because they could not cross rice paddy dikes and similar obstacles. Sometimes the platoon mortars were concentrated into a troop section.

In airborne and airmobile platoons the ACAVs were substituted with ¼-ton M151A1 trucks with M60 machine guns ("gun jeeps"), and the tanks were substituted with 106mm RRs on jeeps. The airborne rifle squad was carried in two jeeps with trailers and the 81mm mortar squad carried in a jeep and trailer. In the airmobile troop these two squads each had a ¼-ton truck, the latter with a trailer. Separate armored cav troops were similarly manned and equipped depending on the type of brigade. Of course, in Vietnam, platoons and their vehicles were somewhat different with many variants.

The air cav troop consisted of an aeroscout platoon with five or six scout helicopters, an aeroweapons platoon with five or six Huey gunships, and an aerorifle platoon with five Huey slicks (troop carriers) in a lift section plus four nine-man rifle squads, each with an M60 and two M79s. Often this platoon was split into two: aerorifle and lift platoons. As with all else, over time the numbers and types of helicopters varied between units.

The armored cavalry regiment (TO&E 17-51) was normally a corps reconnaissance and covering force. The 11th ACR operated as a separate mounted "brigade" on III CTZ's favorable terrain, mainly conducting route clearance and security missions. The regiment consisted of an HHT (TO&E 17-52), an air cav troop (TO&E 17-58), and three squadrons (TO&E 17-55), each with an HHT, three armored cav troops, a tank company (17x M48A3), and a 155mm howitzer battery (6x M109) plus attachments typical of a separate

The Sheridan tank
The M551 armored reconnaissance airborne assault vehicle, commonly called a "light tank," was fielded in 1967. Nine were assigned to Troop H, 1st Cavalry of the 11th InfBde in January 1969, with the first units to be equipped being the 1-11th ACR and 3/4th Cavalry. By 1970 it had replaced M48A3 tanks in most armored cavalry units. The Sheridan had light aluminum armor, was amphibious with preparation, and was parachute droppable. It was armed with a unique 152mm (5.98in.) M81 gun/missile launcher that could fire HEAT-T-multipurpose and massive flechette rounds plus the MGM-51 Shillelagh wire-guided antitank missile, which was not used in Vietnam. There was also a 7.62mm M73 coaxial machine gun and a .50cal M2 atop the turret. The four-man crew had a commander, gunner, loader, and driver. The 300hp diesel engine could drive the 17-ton vehicle to 45mph and had a 285-mi cruising range.

Divisional and nondivisional cavalry squadrons				
Squadron			**Strength**	**TO&E**
Armored Cavalry Squadron, Inf or ArmdDiv			45-22-749	17-105E
	HHT		18-3-199	17-106E
	Armored Cavalry Troop (x3)		6-0-146	17-107E
	Air Cavalry Troop		12-19-112	17-108E
Armored Cavalry Squadron, AbnDiv			40-31-518	17-75F
	HHT		16-2-141	17-76F
	Armored Cavalry Troop (x2)		5-0-125	17-77F
	Air Cavalry Troop		14-29-127	17-78F
Air Cavalry Squadron, Ambl Div			78-96-596	17-95T
	HHT		19-6-157	17-96T
	Air Cavalry Troop (x3)		18-30-104	17-98T
	Armored Cavalry Troop		5-0-127	17-99T

Note:
Strength figures are listed as: Officers-Warrant Officers-Enlisted.

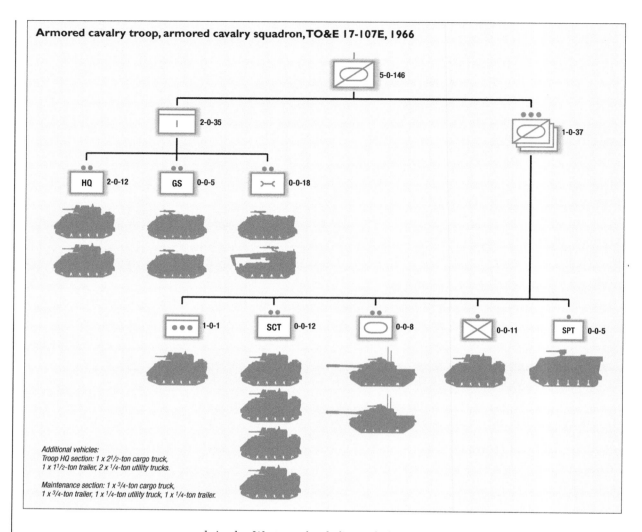

Armored cavalry troop, armored cavalry squadron, TO&E 17-107E, 1966

5-0-146

2-0-35

1-0-37

HQ 2-0-12

GS 0-0-5

0-0-18

1-0-1

SCT 0-0-12

0-0-8

0-0-11

SPT 0-0-5

Additional vehicles:
Troop HQ section: 1 x 2¹/₂-ton cargo truck,
1 x 1¹/₂-ton trailer, 2 x ¹/₄-ton utility trucks.

Maintenance section: 1 x ³/₄-ton cargo truck,
1 x ³/₄-ton trailer, 1 x ¹/₄-ton utility truck, 1 x ¹/₄-ton trailer.

brigade. Westmoreland directed that most of the 11th ACR's 132 tanks be replaced by ACAVs before deployment. The regiment had 51x M48A3 tanks, 296x M113A1 ACAVs and APCs, 18x 155mm M109 SP howitzers, 27x 4.2in. M106A1 mortar carriers, 9x M132A1 mechanized flamethrowers, and 48 scout, troop lift, and armed helicopters. In January 1969 Sheridan tanks began to replace the M48A3s.

11th Armored Cavalry Regiment subunit designations
HHT, 11th ACR
1st Squadron – HHT, Trps A–C, Co D (Tank), Howitzer Btry
2nd Squadron – HHT, Trps E–G, Co H (Tank), Howitzer Btry
3rd Squadron – HHT, Trps I, K, L; Co M (Tank), Howitzer Btry (no Trp J)
Air Cav Trp, 11th ACR
Note:
Howitzer batteries were designated, for example, Howitzer Btry, 1st Sqdn, 11th ACR.

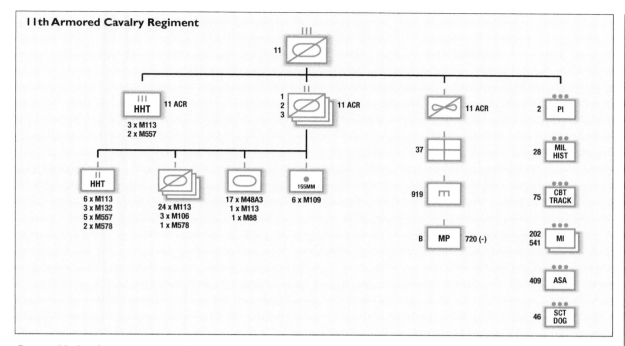

11th Armored Cavalry Regiment

HHT 11 ACR
3 x M113
2 x M557

1 2 3 11 ACR

11 ACR

2 PI

37

28 MIL HIST

HHT
6 x M113
3 x M132
5 x M557
2 x M578

24 x M113
3 x M106
1 x M578

17 x M48A3
1 x M113
1 x M88

155MM
6 x M109

919

75 CBT TRACK

B MP 720 (-)

202 541 MI

409 ASA

46 SCT DOG

Small infantry units

The nature of the Vietnam War saw the need for small, specialized infantry units. Infantry platoons (scout dog) (TO&E 7-167), were organized into a headquarters (commander, platoon sergeant, veterinary technician, and clerk) and four six-man squads. The squads were purely administrative: squad leaders were also dog handlers, as the 24 teams (handler and German shepherd) were attached to rifle companies. They typically walked near the point and utilized silent alerts to detect mines, booby traps, snipers, and other enemy personnel. A platoon was attached to each brigade, with 22 platoons deployed from June 1966, the last arriving in April 1969.

Originally, combat tracker teams (CTT) 1–14 were deployed in April 1966, each with two or four subteams. Four subteam CTTs were attached to divisions, and the two subteam CTTs were attached to separate brigades. They were secretly trained by the New Zealand SAS at the British Jungle Warfare School, Malaysia. On February 9, 1968, they were redesignated as infantry platoons (combat tracker) and infantry detachments (combat tracker) for attachment to divisions and brigades, respectively. The seven division platoons consisted of a headquarters (commander, sergeant, and clerk) and four combat tracker teams. A team (formerly a subteam) had a team leader, a dog handler, a labrador retriever, a visual tracker, and two cover men, one being the RTO. The four two-team detachments for separate brigades had only two teams without a headquarters, although an NCO was detailed to lead it. Their primary mission was to re-establish lost contact with withdrawing enemy forces, such as ambush, rocket-firing, or mining parties. The team would be held at a firebase and helicoptered in to take up the trail where it had been lost or at the site from which it had operated.

The infantry pathfinder platoon (airborne) (TO&E 7-168) consisted of a headquarters with the platoon commander, sergeant, and four 15-man sections with a commander, assistant commander, section sergeant, assistant section sergeant, and 11 pathfinders. A section could operate in two to four teams as required. Aviation battalions were supposed to have a pathfinder detachment, one of the above 15-man sections, but few did. pathfinders were essentially tactical air traffic controllers.

To aid in locating enemy elements, field forces, divisions, and separate brigades were provided LRP units. Initially some divisions and brigades formed their own small LRP detachments. Formal LRP units were authorized in late 1967. Brigades received a 61-man infantry LRP detachment (a platoon), divisions received a 118-man company (two platoons), and field forces received a 198-man (three platoons) or a 230-man company (four platoons). The companies also had a communications platoon. A patrol platoon consisted of eight six-man "patrols" or "recon teams" with a patrol leader, assistant, two scout-observers, and two radio operators. Depending on the mission, they may have operated in 6–14-man teams. On January 1, 1968, the five detachments and nine companies were redesignated Infantry Airborne Ranger companies (TO&E 7-157E) of the 75th Infantry (Companies C–P [no Company J]). They remained their original strength and organization. Regardless of the Ranger designation, they still conducted LRP operations.[5]

Artillery units

Field artillery was critical for fire support of units in the field, firebases, military facilities, and friendly communities. A total of 63 towed and SP 105mm, 155mm, 175mm, and 8in. battalions served in Vietnam. There were also four separate 105mm batteries, five target acquisition batteries (TO&E 6-575)[6], two aerial rocket battalions and two batteries (rocket-firing helicopters), and two aviation batteries (observation helicopters). These units were assigned to field force/corps and division artillery, separate brigades, and five artillery groups. Air defense artillery units also served in Vietnam: three 40mm SP automatic weapons battalions, four .50cal quad SP machine-gun batteries, four searchlight batteries[7], and two HAWK missile battalions (the latter under an air defense group, which never fired a missile in anger; composed of 24 three-rail launchers).

Howitzer and gun battalions were similarly organized regardless of caliber. The HHSB had a battery headquarters that included operation and fire direction, administrative, service, liaison, and medical sections plus a communications and a supply and maintenance platoon. The three howitzer or gun batteries had a battery headquarters, communications, and ammunition sections plus an element known as the firing battery with a headquarters under the XO and four or six howitzer/gun sections. The crew included the section chief (SSG), gunner (SGT), assistant gunner (CPL), and driver (truck or SP mount), with the remainder being cannoneers. SP sections also had a 6-ton M548 ammunition carrier driver. Airmobile 105mm howitzer sections had no prime mover relying completely on helicopters.

All field artillery battalions had three batteries with the exception of infantry division 155mm/8in. howitzer battalions, which had three 155mm towed howitzer batteries and one battery of 8in. SP howitzers. Towed and SP 105mm and 155mm howitzer batteries had six tubes. Eight-inch SP howitzer and 175mm SP gun batteries had four tubes. All 175mm and 8in. battalions were converted to dual-role by early 1969 and had a varied mix of tubes.

Frequently 105mm battalions formed a provisional Battery D that may have been maintained for either a prolonged period or only for short missions. Two howitzers were drawn from two batteries. Crews were smaller and headquarters personnel were drawn from headquarters battery and other howitzer batteries. However, there were shortages of fire direction equipment and field cooking ranges. One unique battery was Battery D (Provisional), 2nd Battalion (105mm towed), 13th Artillery of II FFV Artillery. Known as the "Jungle Battery," it had three 105mm and three 155mm howitzers and supported Special Forces on detached missions in III and IV CTZ.

---

5 See Osprey Elite 13, US Army Rangers and LRRP Units 1942–87.
6 AN/MPQ-4A countermortar radar and AN/TPS-25 ground surveillance radar; replaced by the AN/TPS-58.
7 The 18x 30in. trailer-mounted carbon arc searchlights were replaced by 36x23in. AN/MSS-3 125,000,000-candlepower xenon jeep-mounted searchlights in February 1967. Xenon operated in visible light and infrared modes.

Automatic weapons battalions (40mm SP) (TO&E 44-85) were organized into four batteries with two eight-gun platoons, each with four two-gun sections – 64 Dusters, 16 per battery. A battery was usually attached to a division including non-ARVN allies. Quad .50cal machine-gun batteries (TO&E 44-58) had three eight-gun platoons divided into four two-gun sections –

Nondivisional artillery battalions

Battalion	TO&E	Number
105mm towed howitzer	6-405	5
155mm towed howitzer	6-425	8
105mm SP howitzer	6-415	2
155mm SP howitzer[1]	6-455	4
175mm SP gun[2]	6-435	5
8in. SP howitzer[2]	6-445	5
40mm SP auto weapons	44-85	3
HAWK missile	44-235	2

Divisional/brigade artillery battalions

Battalion	TO&E	Number
105mm howitzer, InfDiv[3]	6-155	12/15
105mm howitzer, Lt InfBde[4]	6-117	4/1
105mm howitzer, AbnDiv/Bde[5]	6-215	5/2
105mm howitzer, AmblDiv[6]	6-705	3/6
155mm SP howitzer, MechBde	6-365	1
155mm/8in. howitzer, InfDiv	6-165	5
Aerial rocket artillery, AmblDiv	6-725	2

Notes:
1 One battalion converted to 175mm/8in. in 1970.
2 When converted to combined 175mm/8in., they retained their original TO&E number.
3 Fifteen, inclusive of three converted from three light infantry brigade battalions in 1969.
4 Four, inclusive of three converted to standard infantry divisional battalions in 1969.
5 Five, inclusive of three converted to airmobile battalions in 1969.
6 Six, inclusive of three converted from airborne battalions in 1969.

105mm howitzer battery, artillery battalion, TO&E 6-157E, 1966

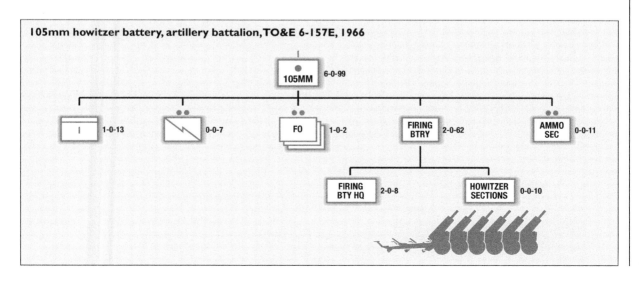

24 "gun trucks." Gun trucks could not be helicopter lifted to firebases, but M55 gun mounts, actually two-wheel trailers, could. Quad .50cal batteries and searchlight (TO&E 6-558) batteries were usually attached to 40mm battalions. These units operated completely splintered with sections attached to infantry, cavalry, and armor units all over the country, providing base defense, supporting sweeps, and escorting convoys.

Line-up of air defense units, 1969

40mm battalion	.50-cal battery	Searchlight battery	Supported
1st Bn, 44th Arty	Btry G, 65th Arty	Btry G, 29th Arty	I CTZ & Marines
5th Bn, 2nd Arty	Btry D, 71st Arty	Btry I, 29th Arty	III & IV CTZ
4th Bn, 60th Arty	Btry E, 41st Arty	Btry B, 29th Arty	II CTZ
	Btry G, 55th Arty		AMERICAL Div
		Btry H, 29th Arty	9th InfDiv

Other units

Engineer units played an important role providing building, facilities, road, and airfield construction and repair; utilities support; water purification; and demolitions. They built just about anything, augmented by contracted construction firms, including highways, bases, airfields, seaports, petroleum storage facilities, among others. Nondivisional engineer units were under the control of US Army Engineer Command, Vietnam. The 18th Engineer Brigade supervised units in I and II CTZ while 20th Engineer Brigade did the same in III and IV CTZ. Each brigade had two or three engineer construction groups with a varying number of engineer battalions and companies attached. The 15 construction battalions built all manner of structures – buildings, bridges, airfields, and pipelines – and paved roads. The 13 combat battalions were lighter equipped and capable of simple building and facility construction, repairing roads and bridges, rehabilitating airfields, etc. The seven divisional combat battalions performed similar missions, but they spent a great deal of time building airstrips, helipads, installing barriers around bases, maintaining and repairing roads, clearing helicopter landing zones, clearing roads of mines, and performing other services. There were also 61 separate engineer companies that were attached to battalions and groups as necessary. These included construction support, port construction, land clearing, dump truck, light equipment, pipeline construction, float bridge, panel bridge, maintenance, and supply, among others.

Military police units were under the 18th MP Brigade with the 16th MP Group responsible for I and II CTZ and the 89th Group responsible for III CTZ and IV CTZ. The 8th MP Group handled the Criminal Investigation Division. Seven MP battalions dealt with security, traffic control, prisoners of war, criminal investigations, and convoy escort. There were 19 separate MP companies of different types. Divisions had an organic MP company while separate brigades had an MP platoon in the HHC.

Aviation units were absolutely critical to US operations for reconnaissance, security, combat and administrative transport, fire support, logistics, command and control, and medical evacuation. Nondivisional aviation units were under the 1st Aviation Brigade with five groups, plus two groups in the airmobile divisions.

Altogether there were 28 divisional and nondivisional aviation battalions and over 140 separate companies.[8] These were exclusive of air cavalry and

8 See Osprey Elite 154, *Vietnam Airmobile Warfare Tactics*.

aerial rocket artillery units. Space does not allow adequate coverage of the aviation organization.

Divisional aviation units should be addressed however. The aviation battalion's airmobile company (light) (latter an air assault company) had 25x UH-1 utility helicopters while the general support company had 10x OH-13/-6 observation helicopters and four OV-1 Mohawk surveillance aircraft. The types of aircraft changed during the war and varied between units. The divisional brigade HHCs had 6x OH-13/-6s, and the DIVARTY HHB had ten. The armored cavalry squadron's air cav troop had 17x UH-1s for troop lift, gunship, and utility duties plus 9x OH-13/-6 scouts.

"Corps" troops

The Army established three corps-level commands in Vietnam: I and II Field Forces, Vietnam and XXIV Corps. These are discussed in the "Command, control, communications and intelligence" chapter. Their organization varied and changed over time, especially with regard to divisions and separate brigades, which could be moved about the country.

Corps-equivalent commands

Unit	I Field Forces	II Field Forces	XXIV Corps
HHC FFV/Corps	I FFV	II FFV	XXIV Corps
FFV/Corps Arty	I FFV	II FFV	XXIV Corps
Artillery Groups	41st, 52nd	23rd, 54th	108th
Aviation Group	17th	12th	62nd Aviation Co
Air Cavalry Sqdn	7-17th Cav	3-17th Cav	--
Signal Battalion	54th	53rd	--
ASA Battalion	313th	303rd (- Co A)	--
PYOPS Battalion	8th	6th	7th
Civil Affairs Co	41st	2nd	29th
Military Police Co	272nd	552nd	A(-)/504th MP Bn
Transportation Co	297th	9th	108th
MI Det	55th	219th	204th
Chemical Det	1st	29th	33rd/48th
Military History Det	13th	7th	31st
Public Info Det	5th/11th	16th	21st
Army Postal Unit	43rd	44th	574th
Divisions[1]	1st Cav, 1st Inf	1st, 9th, & 25th Inf, 1st Cav, 101st Abn	23rd Inf, 101st Abn, 3rd Marine
Brigades[1]	173rd Abn, 3rd Bde/ 25th Inf, 1st Bde/ 101st Abn, Task Force South	173rd Abn, 196th Inf, 199th Inf, 3rd Bde/ 82nd Abn, 3rd Bde/ 101st Abn	196th Inf, 1st Bde/ 5th Inf, 3rd Bde/82nd Abn

Note:
1 Division and brigade assignments were shifted between Field Forces, Vietnam and XXIV Corps. The listed units were not simultaneously assigned to an FFV/corps.

Tactics

Terrain and climate very much affected tactics in Vietnam, at all echelons and especially at the small-unit level. Operations conducted over large areas without front lines were a major departure from conventional tactics employed with identifiable front lines, unit sectors, battle zones, and rear areas. Instead, units were assigned tactical areas of responsibility (TAOR) and areas of operation (AO). The front line was the direction in which one faced at any one time. Units moved into these areas by foot, via helicopter, on APCs, or aboard riverine assault craft. They conducted short-term operations attempting to locate, engage, and destroy the enemy. They did not attempt to hold ground other than securing major population centers and their own bases.

US conventional tactics had actually changed little from World War II. Units from divisions down to platoons were organized into three subunits with a fire support element. On a conventional battlefield they deployed with two subunits online and one in reserve – "two up, one back." This generally applied to a linear defense or the attack. The Army practised a linear defense with an armored and air cavalry in the covering force area screening the forward edge of the battle area – the main line of resistance. Behind this main battle area were mobile reserve, artillery, and support and service units. Units were resupplied daily using main supply routes. In the offense units advanced mainly on high-speed avenues of approach (roads and highways) closely followed by artillery and support. Rather than orienting on enemy forces, as in conventional tactics, they focused on terrain. Whoever controlled key terrain features, including main roads, bridges, and other points, dominated the battlefield.

Little of this was applicable in Vietnam. Rather than being assigned relatively narrow defense sectors or attack zones, divisions with a 12–18-mi frontage were given a TAOR of 2,000–5,000 sq mi as opposed to a 200–300-sq mi zone on a conventional battlefield. An example of a small TAOR is one of 2,400 sq mi measured at roughly 40x60 mi. Most divisions had even larger TAORs.

There were no front lines or rear areas. Divisions would build a major base – "the rear" – that they might occupy for many months or years, if not for their entire tour. One or more brigades would be based there along with some of the divisional and attached artillery, especially long-range pieces. Divisional and nondivisional aviation, combat support, and service units were based there as well. These semipermanent bases eventually boasted barracks, support facilities, headquarters buildings, an airstrip, and even clubs and outdoor movie theaters. One or two brigades may have had their own bases in more critical areas of the TAOR. These could also be permanent or semipermanent with much the same facilities as the division base. Battalions rotated to the bases for security and rest.

Doctrine calls for every unit to be able to defend itself whether it was a combat unit or an administrative unit. Division bands provided CP security. Most units were responsible for their own security, and infantry units were not attached for security. If they had been, there would have been few units available to conduct combat operations.

These bases were supplied by helicopter and fixed-wing transports if they had an airstrip, but most supplies were delivered by road convoy due to the large amounts required. Transportation truck companies, conducting convoys to bases, were well armed. One truck company was stood down, and pairs of trucks were reassigned to other companies – in order not to reduce the company's haulage capacity – armed with quad .50s. The guns would be placed at either end of the company convoy and in the middle of a platoon convoy, and some other trucks were armed with M60s. Two XM706 (V-100) light armored cars or M60-armed "gun jeeps" from MP escort companies might also accompany convoys.

Brigades and battalions were assigned TAORs within the division TAOR. These would change as operations were redirected and as responses were made to intelligence and enemy activity. Field forces, divisions, and brigades could conduct multi-unit operations in specific areas, often including other Free World forces, usually for a specified period. Thousands of such operations were conducted and assigned codenames. Each operation was assigned a specific AO.

Divisions with 9–11 maneuver battalions and significant artillery and combat support units could influence the battle and shift forces to support engaged units. One would think a separate brigade with three or four maneuver battalions would have had one-third the combat power of a division, but this was not the case. It did not have the assets common to a division to reinforce multiple engaged units.

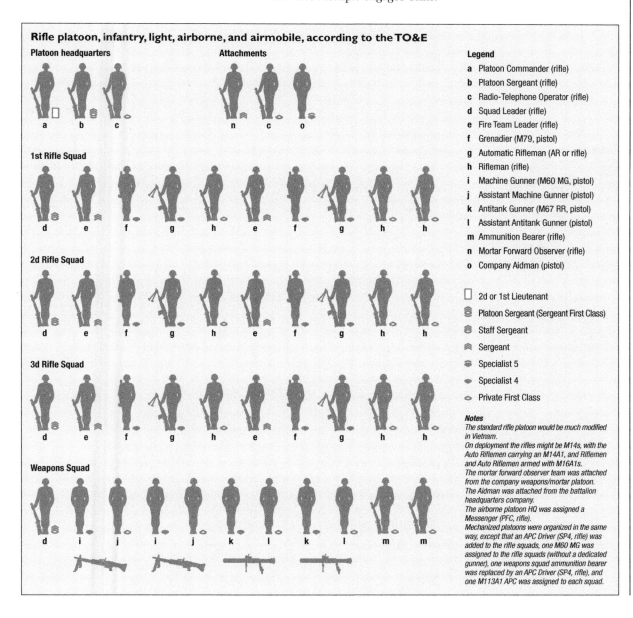

Rifle platoon, infantry, light, airborne, and airmobile, according to the TO&E

Platoon headquarters
a   b   c

Attachments
n   c   o

1st Rifle Squad
d   e   f   g   h   e   f   g   h   h

2d Rifle Squad
d   e   f   g   h   e   f   g   h   h

3d Rifle Squad
d   e   f   g   h   e   f   g   h   h

Weapons Squad
d   i   j   i   j   k   l   k   l   m   m

Legend

a   Platoon Commander (rifle)
b   Platoon Sergeant (rifle)
c   Radio-Telephone Operator (rifle)
d   Squad Leader (rifle)
e   Fire Team Leader (rifle)
f   Grenadier (M79, pistol)
g   Automatic Rifleman (AR or rifle)
h   Rifleman (rifle)
i   Machine Gunner (M60 MG, pistol)
j   Assistant Machine Gunner (pistol)
k   Antitank Gunner (M67 RR, pistol)
l   Assistant Antitank Gunner (pistol)
m   Ammunition Bearer (rifle)
n   Mortar Forward Observer (rifle)
o   Company Aidman (pistol)

☐   2d or 1st Lieutenant
    Platoon Sergeant (Sergeant First Class)
    Staff Sergeant
    Sergeant
    Specialist 5
    Specialist 4
    Private First Class

Notes
The standard rifle platoon would be much modified in Vietnam.
On deployment the rifles might be M14s, with the Auto Riflemen carrying an M14A1, and Riflemen and Auto Riflemen armed with M16A1s.
The mortar forward observer team was attached from the company weapons/mortar platoon.
The Aidman was attached from the battalion headquarters company.
The airborne platoon HQ was assigned a Messenger (PFC, rifle).
Mechanized platoons were organized in the same way, except that an APC Driver (SP4, rifle) was added to the rifle squads, one M60 MG was assigned to the rifle squads (without a dedicated gunner), one weapons squad ammunition bearer was replaced by an APC Driver (SP4, rifle), and one M113A1 APC was assigned to each squad.

The primary maneuver unit was the battalion. Typically a battalion established a fire support base from which to operate. A rifle company defended most bases. At least one 105mm howitzer battery was positioned there, but it might have included a second 105mm battery or a 155mm howitzer battery, or perhaps just two or three 155mm howitzers.

Whether called a fire support base (FSB), firebase (FB), combat base, or landing zone (LZ), these sites varied greatly in layout, mission, and duration.[9] Many were virtually permanent, providing security along critical lines of communications. Most were established for just a few weeks or months to support an operation. They might be reoccupied later to support further operations, but they would have had to be completely rebuilt because they were leveled when abandoned. Some firebases were in place for only days. An LZ usually identified a very short-term firebase. Often this was a helicopter LZ in which troops were inserted for an operation. But rather than merely being delivered and on their way, an artillery battery was emplaced and the deployed companies were supplied from the LZ by helicopter delivery. The LZ would be closed and relocated elsewhere as the infantry units moved. Even shorter-term LZs were established during artillery raids. The LZ would be secured, two to six artillery pieces would be delivered, fire missions shot, and then the artillery was lifted out to another hilltop. To support planned operations, firebases would be established in advance, around and within the AO to provide overlapping artillery coverage. Units simply did not operate from under the artillery umbrella. Besides complete coverage of the AO, the ability to direct fire from different directions prevented artillery from being masked in some areas by hills and ridges. Longer-ranged 155mm, 175mm, and 8in. artillery would provide additional support from afar. Besides extensive artillery, which reduced the need for mortars, heavy reliance was placed on attack helicopters and close air support by fighter bombers.

9 See Osprey Fortifications 58, *Vietnam Firebases 1965–73: American and Australian Forces.*

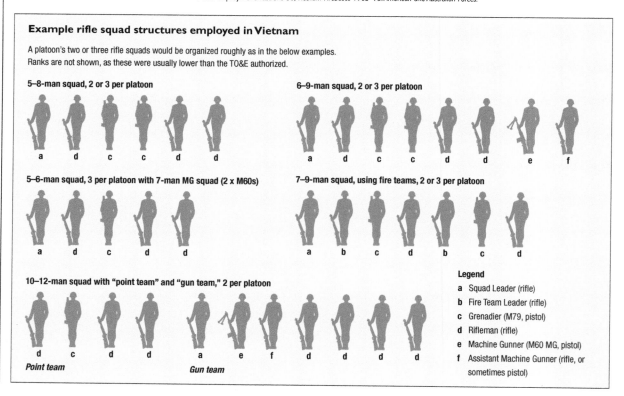

Example rifle squad structures employed in Vietnam

A platoon's two or three rifle squads would be organized roughly as in the below examples.
Ranks are not shown, as these were usually lower than the TO&E authorized.

5–8-man squad, 2 or 3 per platoon

a d c c d d

6–9-man squad, 2 or 3 per platoon

a d c c d d e f

5–6-man squad, 3 per platoon with 7-man MG squad (2 x M60s)

a d c d d

7–9-man squad, using fire teams, 2 or 3 per platoon

a b c d b c d

10–12-man squad with "point team" and "gun team," 2 per platoon

d c d d a e f d d d d
Point team   *Gun team*

Legend

a Squad Leader (rifle)
b Fire Team Leader (rifle)
c Grenadier (M79, pistol)
d Rifleman (rifle)
e Machine Gunner (M60 MG, pistol)
f Assistant Machine Gunner (rifle, or sometimes pistol)

The extensive helicopter support available added a capability that greatly changed tactics and allowed units to operate over large areas and bypass terrain obstacles. Here a UH-1H Huey lands at a firebase.

Typical mechanized rifle platoon as employed in Vietnam

Squad organization all but disappeared, and the platoon's troops became "track crews." This is one example, but other variations were used. Ranks are not shown, as these were usually lower than the TO&E authorized.

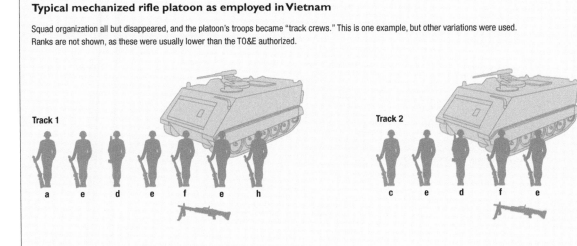

Track 1
a e d e f e h

Track 2
c e d f e

Track 3
c e d f e

Track 4
b e d f e i

Legend

a Platoon Commander (rifle)
b Platoon Sergeant (rifle)
c Squad Leader (rifle)

d Grenadier (M79, pistol)
e Rifleman (rifle)
f Machine Gunner (M60 MG, pistol)

g APC Driver
h Mortar Forward Observer (rifle)
i Company Aidman (pistol)

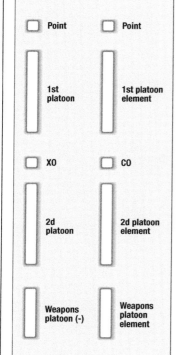

The goal was simply to destroy enemy forces, disrupt their logistics and communications, and neutralize the VC infrastructure, the shadow government of the VC that was overlaid on the RVN government administration. The control of population centers, lines of communications, and resources was important, of course, but US forces served as mobile forces searching for enemy main forces. Some units may have operated outside major population centers to reinforce their security, but actual defense was left largely to ARVN and Regional and Popular Forces. US forces possessed the necessary mobility, firepower, and logistical assets for this role.

There were occasional battles over a piece of terrain such as the 173rd AbnBde's Hill 875 in November 1967 and the 101st AbnDiv's Hamburger Hill in May 1969. US units were also called to retake portions of cities, especially notable during February 1968 in Saigon and Hue. Mostly however the operations were search and destroy missions intended to defeat enemy forces, destroy facilities, and evacuate supplies and materials. Owing to media criticism, this term was replaced by search and clear. Search and secure operations were to sweep an area and establish local security to deny the area to the enemy. This was usually an area in which civilian populations were found. It was important that the enemy be denied access to civilians to prevent the populace from being exploited for recruitment, labor, taxes, and food. These missions were performed mostly by infantry, although mech, armor, and cavalry units participated. These latter units, while capable of cross-country movement in some areas, did not possess the stealthiness of infantry to operate effectively on dense and rugged terrain against an elusive enemy. They were more effective for security missions such as clearing and securing roads and highways, bases, and population centers. These missions could be temporary in nature or of long duration to secure key lines of communications.

Battalions usually deployed with three companies in the "bush." They were often separated by some distance, searching separate areas, with the scout platoon operating independently as well. The scout platoon might have been in support of one of the companies or at least near to one in case the small platoon was engaged. One company secured the firebase, but it did not serve as a reaction force. That would be handled by one of the other companies or more likely a company detailed from another battalion, sitting on standby at an airstrip. The companies might be given specific areas to search, a route to follow, or an objective to move to where suspected enemy might be found. If a company was engaged, artillery, gunship, and close air support would be provided as required. Other companies on the ground might be ordered to support the company and/or helicopter reaction forces could be dispatched to land on nearby LZs.

Companies moved in as dispersed formations as the terrain permitted. In dense vegetation this might be a single file, the "long green line." In lighter vegetation a company moved in two parallel columns within sight of each other. If flank security was used at all, it was within sight as well. In flank security, soldiers had to break their own trail, which made more noise and slowed them down. Additionally, it exposed them to the risk of being mistaken for enemy or becoming separated from the rest of the company. Rear security was essential. Ambushes were left on the back trail to hit any enemy that may be following. In more open areas, as in the Central Highlands, platoons would deploy on line or in wedge formations (an inverted "V") in clearings that were too large to skirt, such as rice paddies. When crossing linear obstacles such as roads, gullies, streams, small swamps, and other restrictive features that slowed down troops, the bulk of the unit would have to slow to a crawl or halt altogether to allow the rest of the unit to catch up.

When halted for rest breaks, a perimeter would be formed and security outposts established at a short distance. An ambush might be set up on the back trail, and other ambushes might be set too, one in the morning and another in the afternoon. Before dark, units halted to eat, but ideally they

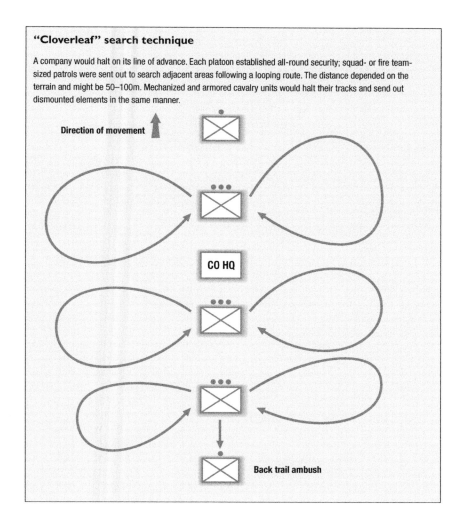

"Cloverleaf" search technique

A company would halt on its line of advance. Each platoon established all-round security; squad- or fire team-sized patrols were sent out to search adjacent areas following a looping route. The distance depended on the terrain and might be 50–100m. Mechanized and armored cavalry units would halt their tracks and send out dismounted elements in the same manner.

Direction of movement

CO HQ

Back trail ambush

moved to their night position at dusk, making it difficult for the enemy to pinpoint their location. At night, companies coiled into tight perimeters, in a "remain overnight" (RON) position. Listening posts were seldom deployed as they were exposed and cut off if the enemy attacked. Artillery concentrations were plotted around the RON. Units generally received a minor resupply ("resup") by helicopter every three days, mainly rations and mail. Every six days a major resup was delivered. A hot meal might even be flown in. Damaged equipment and clothing were exchanged, replacements delivered, and men were flown in and out for R&R and to return home. This was often a day of rest, and the unit moved only to change its RON. Two helicopter lifts might arrive.

The battalion forward command post was set up in a firebase, and the company rear was there as well. The "sick, lame, and lazy" and new replacements assisted with security and work details while the company XO or first sergeant dealt with admin and resupply. Besides a rifle company the battalion HHC and CSC elements also provided security and never-ending work details; digging positions and drainage ditches; filling sandbags; stringing concertina wire; KP; burning out latrines; and loading and unloading supplies, ammunition, and construction materials from helicopters.

Larger-scale operations were conducted with the battalion concentrated to clear a larger area or secure an objective. Cordon operations required multiple companies, often more than a battalion. For example, a village or an area suspected of containing an enemy unit might be cordoned, or surrounded.

A small firebase surrounded by a large cleared field of fire. Note that the perimeter fighting bunkers are arranged in clusters. In the center is the large tactical operations center (TOC). Firebases allowed the emplacement of artillery that could cover units operating in the field.

Some of these areas might be quite large. No continuous line could be deployed. A determined enemy breakout would overrun a thin line, even platoon positions. Instead, companies were deployed around the area in single positions, often resulting in hundreds of meters-wide gaps, if not several kilometers-wide holes. Ambushes might set out at night, but the enemy was adept at infiltrating out of such traps.

Many contacts were by chance with two moving elements colliding. Whichever side detected the other first had the advantage of either moving into position to execute an ambush or at least opening fire first. If a small force was engaged or if it engaged a larger force, it would attempt to break contact as soon as possible. The larger force, besides having more firepower, would attempt to outflank or encircle the smaller.

Regardless of the unit's size, a point man was deployed. He searched for signs of the enemy, booby traps, and mines. Another rifleman or grenadier closely followed him. Only the most alert, experienced men "ran point." More riflemen and a machine-gun team followed. If engaged, the point man would empty his magazine on full-automatic and fall back as grenadiers, riflemen, and machine gunners opened fire. Units would attempt to gain fire superiority as rapidly as possible by moving subunits into position and calling for fire

A rifle company of the 1st CavDiv (Ambl) debark from a landing craft, utility (LCU) after being ferried from their troop transport. They are still equipped with M1956 web gear with bedrolls and butt packs, equipment totally inadequate for Vietnam.

support. Not only would men and weapons have to be pushed forward, but the flanks and rear had to be secured. To assume the enemy was only in front of one could be a fatal mistake. A firefight might only last for minutes, the "seven-minute war," or it could turn into a major action when two patrols collided and the respective commanders committed additional units.

Any commander on the ground was restricted to the same limited visibility as his troops. This was often measured in meters. For this reason battalion commanders and higher commanders often appeared over the action aboard command and control helicopters, controlling and coordinating the operation's many moving pieces. The S3 (operations) officer and artillery and aviation liaison officers accompanied him. This system was often criticized on the grounds that the commander might lose the "feel for the ground," losing touch with the ground time-distance factor and urging his company commanders to achieve unrealistic speeds and actions. From the air, distances seemed inconsequential, and the rough terrain hidden by trees was not appreciated. Commanders could sometimes forget that the men were heavily loaded, exhausted, stressed, and possibly low on water. For those commanders who could retain a realistic perspective, being in the air was a better place to be for command and control purposes rather than struggling through dense vegetation and unable to see beyond 10–20 m (roughly 30–70 ft). Units on the ground marked their positions by various means and then indicated the enemy's distance and direction. An

"Jitterbug saturation" patrolling technique

A battalion would helicopter-insert platoons from two companies plus the reconnaissance platoon in designated search areas. The third company secured a nearby firebase, providing artillery support, and the fourth company was on standby alert at an airstrip as a reaction force, or could also be used to block enemy troops fleeing the search zone. Landing zones were plotted throughout the area on which the reaction force might be inserted. Search platoons would spend a day or two searching their areas and then move by foot or air to another. Such moves could be randomly dictated, or be in response to enemy movements detected by scout helicopters also searching the zone. This is a representative diagram only: the area might be more irregular, with terrain features used for the boundaries.

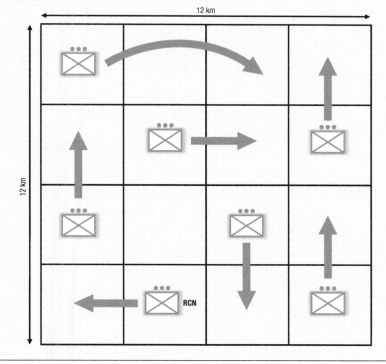

A rifle squad leader carries a pair of Ho Chi Minh sandals. The growing shortage of NCOs led to many squad leaders being one or two grades lower than those authorized.

assistant would plot friendly locations and enemy sightings on a map board. Artillery, gunships, scout helicopters, close air support, medevacs, resupply, and commitment of reserves and reaction forces were all co-ordinated from an aerial vantage point with a very quick response time. The movements of all units on the ground could be orchestrated by the airborne commander.

When attacked by a superior force, day or night, companies coiled into a tight perimeter and artillery, gunships, and close air support were called in. Some of these positions took a beating, some almost caved in, and some were withdrawn on order, but none were ever totally overrun. The same cannot be said for a few platoon perimeters that were overrun. They lacked the firepower to survive against a concerted assault.

Regardless of the type of operation, the employment of helicopters for transportation, reconnaissance, command and control, fire support, resupply, medical evacuation, liaison, and other purposes was critical. The commander of a supporting aviation unit could also be on station to control the many helicopters performing all these tasks.

Tank, mechanized infantry, and armored cavalry units were not as restricted by terrain as might be assumed. There were large areas on which AFVs could operate. They were especially useful for line-of-communications security. It was not uncommon for tank battalions to be splintered into companies and even into platoons for deployment as security forces. There were never enough tanks to go around. Tanks occasionally conducted company- and battalion-sized operations, often in the form of sweeps through fairly dense vegetation. Often with a dozer tank in the lead, they would crash through moderately dense forests. This would create a snaking trail-like path called a "tank bust," which remained for many months and was often used again. The enemy however used them too, for cross-country travel. Mounted units were often employed as blocking forces after positioning themselves on possible escape routes. The tank busts they created even served as kill zones that fleeing enemy would have to cross. The principal threats to tanks and other AFVs were mines, RPG-7s, recoilless rifles, and mud, in that order.

Small-unit tactics were greatly refined in Vietnam, especially with regard to patrols, ambushes, and counterambush. There were other innovations made in co-ordinating fire support, a resurrection of the almost lost art of sniping, convoy security, the use of scout and tracker dogs, and riverine operations. The American soldier proved himself to be extremely innovative in developing new tactics and techniques and adapting the employment of conventional weapons to a tactical environment for which they were not intended.

Patrols conducted by companies included combat and reconnaissance patrols. Combat patrols were intended to engage the enemy. These were mainly security and ambush patrols. Security patrols were short-range missions intended to check an area surrounding the unit and to prevent the enemy from discovering or attacking the unit. These patrols would engage and destroy or drive off the enemy.

Ambushes were established on avenues of approach that led to a unit's position or to a base, the objective being to destroy approaching attackers or patrols. Ambushes were not simply established in the middle of the jungle. Likely approaches in areas of dense vegetation, gullies, and low ground, or any area that would provide the enemy concealment might be selected. They would also be set up on roads, trails, tank busts, stream crossings, and canals (to ambush boat traffic). Most ambushes were of the linear type with the kill force online parallel with the route on which the kill zone was designated. Command-detonated Claymore mines would cover the kill zone along with machine guns. Flank security was established some distance out from both ends of the kill force to warn of the enemy's approach, protect against being outflanked, and to halt any survivors fleeing from the kill zone. Rear security was also provided, and teams were designated to search enemy dead, recover weapons and equipment, and take any prisoners. The deadliest ambush formation was the L-shaped, which positioned a long arm parallel to the ambushed route and a shorter arm perpendicular to the route and enfilading it (firing down the route's long axis). There was also a V-shaped ambush with kill forces on both sides of the route with the "V" pointing up the line of movement. This was usually positioned on a hillside and allowed the kill forces to fire down into the kill zone and not into each other.

Reconnaissance patrols were sent out to reconnoiter specific areas for enemy activity. Such patrols had to be large enough to fight their way out of ambushes and chance contacts. A small patrol could be easily trapped and wiped out if it did not have sufficient manpower and firepower. A common patrolling technique was for a company to halt and establish a perimeter and send out several patrols that would loop out and return on a different route – a "cloverleaf" movement. If only a short distance, a squad reinforced by a machine gun might be sent. Owing to the reduced strength of most squads and to provide sufficient firepower, a platoon was more often dispatched. Ostensibly, reconnaissance patrols were to avoid contact, but because of the short ranges at which the enemy was detected and the driving desire to engage and destroy the enemy, more often than not they were immediately engaged unless the patrol was obviously outnumbered.

Many units developed specialized tactics for specific enemy and terrain situations. These often fell into disuse when the unit moved to a new area with different situations. Subsequently, new techniques were developed. Tactics also changed with the change of commanders.

In the Mekong Delta the VC built bunker lines along canals, often backed by open river paddies. Once these positions were discovered through aerial reconnaissance or when the VC ambushed water traffic, artillery-supported airmobile platoons would be rapidly inserted in numerous points around the area to "seal" it in a process called "jitterbugging." Platoons would be inserted by helicopter at scattered points, taking advantage of the delta's open terrain, and they would establish blocking positions to engage the fleeing enemy. Other helicopters would remain airborne to be directed to insert platoons to pursue enemy forces who may have slipped through.

"Bushmaster" operations saw the insertion of platoons into sparsely vegetated areas in the last two hours of daylight. The platoons occupied ambush positions after dark to interdict VC movement. A central command post was established, and the platoons were positioned within 750m (820 yd) of each other to provide mutual support if one initiated an ambush. An offshoot of the bushmaster was "checkerboard." The next day the platoons would break down into squads, occupying a grid square pattern. Squads moved continuously from square to square to locate small enemy elements. Since it was only a two-day operation, they carried only enough ammunition and rations to allow them to move easily. This technique was practical when the VC separated into small parties to evade the US sweep.

The "Eagle Flight" concept was developed by US advisers with ARVN units in 1962 and was so successful that it was established by later-arriving US units. Normally four or five Hueys were used along with a varied number of gunships and scouts, one or two of each. A rifle platoon with a small squad in four of the Hueys served as the ground element. They conducted aerial search sweeps looking for VC activity. When a small enemy element was detected, the four squads were inserted at different points to box in the enemy and attack them from different directions or prevent them from escaping. These platoons were especially useful in pursuit operations against VC who attacked a Free World base or had executed an ambush and were withdrawing in small groups. Withdrawing enemy would be detected, and squads would be inserted in blocking positions. The command element would remain aloft in the command and control helicopter to detect enemy movement, direct the squads, co-ordinate and direct gunship and artillery fire, and scout beyond the area in which the squads were operating to detect

Battalion operation against a suspected VC base camp

In this example, intelligence has indicated the possible presence of a VC base camp. One company is airmobile-inserted to establish blocking positions to the north. A further two companies are inserted to sweep the suspected base area. One of the companies cordons and searches a village. The scout platoon moves out from a firebase to cover the flank of one of the companies. The fourth company is on standby at a supporting firebase as a reaction force.

enemy reaction forces moving toward the insertion. Eagle Flights were also used to recover friendly dead from the battlefield and to search for individual friendlies separated from their units owing to action. An important mission was to rescue downed helicopter aircrew and recover dead, weapons, radios, sensitive documents, and other items from the aircraft. If the aircraft could not be lifted out by heavy helicopters, they would destroy it with demolitions.

These platoons also flew night missions using new night vision devices to detect and engage VC units moving under the cover of darkness. A command and control helicopter would fly at about 2,500ft dropping flares in areas suspected of harboring VC/NVA. Two gunships would fly at a lower altitude and attack any detected enemy. A later refinement was for one helicopter to fly along at an enticingly high altitude with its running lights on. A gunship would follow at a slightly higher altitude, its sound masked by the lead aircraft. Mounted in the gunship's door were a powerful infrared spotlight and a 3,000rpm 7.62mm M134 Minigun. If the enemy fired on the lead helicopter or were otherwise detected, they would be engaged. Eagle Flights could also direct artillery fire onto the enemy.

These are just some of the many tactical innovations developed by units through the course of the war.

Weapons and equipment

The US Army was well armed and well equipped to conduct conventional or nuclear wars, mainly in Europe. However, it was structured to deploy and fight anywhere in the world in any type of conflict. This meant that its weapons were designed for flexible use, and most of the equipment was light enough to be deployed by air.

Weapons

The standard shoulder weapon was the 7.62mm M14 rifle, a semi-automatic with a 20-round magazine. It was rugged and reliable but rather heavy, as was its ammunition. It was understood that in Vietnam, infantrymen had to carry everything they needed for three to five days, including rations and water, heavier than customary loads in the States and Europe. Lighter weapons were necessary.

Accompanying the M14 was the M14(M) (Modified) automatic rifle with a bipod. Notoriously inaccurate and easily overheated owing to its light barrel, the M14E2 automatic rifle was issued in 1965 and redesignated the M14A1 in 1966. It was fitted with a straight-line stock, muzzle stabilizer, and two pistol grips, but it was still inaccurate and overheated. Another variant of the M14 was the telescoped XM21 sniper rifle fielded in 1969.

An alternative rifle was available however. The 5.56mm XM16E1 "black rifle" replaced the M14 in airborne and air assault units in 1964. The first three Army units deployed to Vietnam in 1965, the 173rd AbnBde; 1st Bde, 101st AbnDiv; and 1st CavDiv (Ambl) were armed with the "black rifle." It had been in use in Vietnam by advisers and Special Forces since 1962. The only divisions deploying with M14s were the 1st and 25th. By August 1966 all Army combat units in Vietnam were issued the XM16E1. In December it was recommended that the M16 replace the M14 in all Army units. The XM16E1 had teething problems, which were largely corrected, and in January 1967 the improved rifles were redesignated the M16A1. The M16A1 had a 20-round magazine, was semi- and full-automatic, and was light. It weighed only 7.6 lb compared with the M14's 9.5 lb, and thus more ammunition could be carried.

There was no 5.56mm squad automatic weapon available to replace the dismal M14A1. A few units retained the M14A1 for a short time, but it fell by the wayside owing to its inadequacies, weight, and different caliber. It was reasoned that since M16A1s were all full-automatic a dedicated automatic rifle was unnecessary. The M16A1, even with a bipod, lacked the necessary range, penetration through cover, and sustained fire capability to be effective in that role. The M16A1 was a good rifle, but it required meticulous cleaning, was comparatively fragile, and had poor penetration through brush, bamboo, sandbags, and earth parapets. Most troops arriving in Vietnam had never seen an M16A1, having used the M14 through Basic Training and Infantry Advanced Individual (AIT) Training. M16A1s were not issued to infantry training centers until late 1969, other than at Ft Gordon, SC, which provided Basic and AIT to infantrymen destined for Parachute School.

The 7.62mm M60 machine gun, or "pig," played an important role since there was no squad automatic weapon. At 23 lb it was heavy, but it put out a high rate of fire that could chop through dense vegetation. It was shoulder- and bipod-fired but could be mounted on an M122 tripod and had a quick-change barrel. Ammunition was provided in 100-round belts, of which any number could be linked together.

One-third of a squad's firepower was found in the 40mm M79 grenade launcher, the "blooper" or "thumper." The M79 could fire high explosive (HE)

An aviator stands beside prefab contract bunker caps. These were helicoptered into firebases and set over pre-dug, pre-sandbagged bits. (Peter J. Dunnev)

Armored cavalry troops of airmobile divisions and airborne and light infantry brigades were equipped with M151A1 "gun jeeps," which proved much more useful, in some areas, than full-tracked armored vehicles.

The crew of a 155mm M14A1 howitzer jacks the weapon up on its jack stand, which allowed it to be traversed. If possible, artillery pieces were mounted on level timber platforms to improve their accuracy.

fragmentation rounds on a small target at 150-plus meters (164-plus yd) and on area targets up to 350m (383 yd). The antipersonnel round (aka "buckshot" or "shotgun" round) was loaded with 20x .13cal No. 4 buckshot effective to 30m (98 ft). It could also launch various colored smoke and pyrotechnic signals and illumination flares. Grenadiers, however, did not carry a rifle, thus reducing point target firepower. The M79s also could not be used in extremely dense brush, negating the grenadier's use. In December 1966 the XM148 grenade launcher began to see field testing in a few units. It was mounted below the M16's hand guard. It proved defective, and so the XM203 began field testing in 1968 and was standardized as the M203 the following year. The M79 remained in wide use throughout the war, however.

Two one-time use weapons saw wide service. The M72 and M72A1 LAWs were 5.2 lb single-shot 66mm rocket launchers with a HEAT warhead. Intended as an antitank weapon, it was less than effective against personnel and bamboo and thatch huts. It was also susceptible to the climate and sometimes failed to fire. Another problem was that if its projectile struck the ground at a low angle, a given because of the flat trajectory, it often failed to detonate. The M72 and M72A1s were used against bunkers and barrage-fired into trees containing snipers. Maximum effective range was 325 m (355 yd).

The M18A1 Claymore antipersonnel mine was a 3.5 lb directional mine in a rectangular, slightly curved fiberglass box. It contained 1.5 lb of C4 plastic explosive backing 704 7⁄32in.-diameter ball bearings, making the Claymore devastating to assaulting troops and those caught in an ambush kill zone. It was electrically detonated by command or it could be rigged with a tripwire to be activated by an intruder. When detonated, the ball bearings were blasted out in a 60-degree fan with an optimum range of 50m (165ft) but dangerous out to 250m (820ft). Blast and secondary fragmentation were dangerous within 100m (328ft) in all directions.

Limited use was made of 12-gauge, pump-action shotguns with 20in. barrels. The most common models were the Remington Model 870, the Ithaca Model 37, the Savage Model 69E, and the Stevens Model 77E, among others. They were fed by six-round tubular magazines and used 00 buckshot (9x .33cal lead balls). Sometimes used by point men, they were mainly used by MPs and prison guards. Their main faults were that they had limited penetration through brush and bamboo and had to be reloaded one round at a time. The standard pistol was the Colt .45cal M1911A1 with a seven-round magazine. Aviators were armed with a Smith & Wesson .38 Special Model 10 revolver.

Browning .50cal M2 machine guns – the "Ma Deuce" – were issued to headquarters and support units. They were not manned by dedicated crews but by support personnel, and they were used for base defense. Other heavy weapons organic to companies and battalions were likewise seldom carried in the field owing to the weapons' and ammunition's weight and bulk and the rugged terrain and harsh climate. The company 81mm M29 and M29A1 mortars weighed 132 lb and could lob HE, white phosphorus (WP), and illumination rounds out to 3,650m (3,992 yd). The M29A1, adopted in 1964, had a chrome-plated bore prolonging barrel life. The "eighty-one" often replaced battalion 4.2in. M30 mortars. Weighing 672 lb the M30, called the "four-deuce," was far too heavy for anything but emplacement in firebases. It had a range of 5,500m (6,015 yd), but its use for base defense was limited as its minimum range was 770m (842 yd). It was used for illumination and firing on possible enemy assembly areas and supporting weapons positions. The "eighty-one's" minimum range was 70 m (77 yd).

A Chinook lands a 105mm howitzer on the Bong Son Plain; in the bottom right, a cannoneer shields his face from the powerful rotor wash of the helicopter's blades.

The 106mm M40A1 recoilless rifle mounted on an M151A1C jeep was another company and battalion weapon of limited use. Its ammunition included HEAT-T (high explosive antitank), HEP-T (high explosive plastic), WP, and antipersonnel tracer (using flechettes, or dart-like, steel projectiles). Some battalions retained a few for firebase defense where they proved to be effective anti-sniper and harassing fire weapons. Most were placed in storage. At 37 lb the rifle platoon's 90mm M67 recoilless rifles were heavy and very seldom taken to the field. Its 9.5 lb HEAT round was marginally effective as an antibunker weapon, and there was a flechette round, but it was simply not worth the effort of carrying the weapon.

Rather than mortars and recoilless rifles, heavy reliance was placed on artillery, attack helicopters, and close air support. The "one-oh-five" or "dime-nickel" was the mainstay divisional artillery piece and separate brigade artillery piece since 1940. It was then that the 105mm M2A1 howitzer was adopted (M1 and M2 never entered series production). The M2A1 was redesignated the M101A1 in 1962. In 1966 (adopted 1964) the lighter 3,017 lb M102 began to replace the 4,980 lb M101A1, but it continued in use through the war. The M101A1 was of conventional design, with a split trail and a large shield. It was towed by a 2$\frac{1}{2}$-ton truck and had an 11,000m (12,030 yd) range. The M102 had an open box

Introduction of major weapons and AFVs in Vietnam

105mm M101A1 towed howitzer[1]	May 1965
90mm M56 Scorpion SP antitank gun[2]	May 1965
4.2in. M106 mortar carrier	May 1965
M113 armored personnel carrier[1]	May 1965
HAWK air defense missile system	September 1965
90mm M48A3 Patton combat tank	October 1965
81mm M125A1 mortar carrier	October 1965
M113A1 armored personnel carrier	October 1965
8in. M110 SP howitzer	October 1965
175mm M107 SP gun	October 1965
155mm M109 SP howitzer	October 1965
155mm M114A1 towed howitzer[1]	October 1965
165mm M728 combat engineer vehicle	November 1965
105mm M102 towed howitzer	March 1966
105mm M108 SP howitzer	June 1966
.50cal M55 SP quad machine gun	October 1966
40mm M42A1 Duster SP AA gun	November 1966
XM706 Commando security vehicle	June 1967
152mm M551 Sheridan light tank	December 1967
90mm M48A2 Patton combat tank[3]	April 1968
20mm XM741 Vulcan SP AA gun	December 1968

Notes:
1 Introduction by US; previously in use by ARVN.
2 Withdrawn mid-1966.
3 Substitute for M48A3.

trail, lacked a shield, and when emplaced was jacked up on a stand allowing it to traverse 360 degrees with the aid of a roller in the trail's end. It could be towed by a $\frac{3}{4}$-ton truck and had an 11,500 m (12,577 yd) range. Both could be sling-loaded beneath a CH-47 helicopter. The M101A1 required three minutes to emplace, and the M102 required four. Ten-man crews could crank out 30rpm for the first three minutes and fire 3rpm indefinitely. Two battalions of 105mm M108 SP howitzers were deployed to Vietnam. These were being phased out because they used the same chassis as the 155mm M109 but had less range and lethality. A 33 lb HE round had a 175m (191 yd) casualty radius. Ammunition included HE, HEAT, HEP-T, WP, burning smoke, illumination, and antipersonnel tracer (called "beehive" rounds because of the whistling buzz they made).

The standard divisional and corps general support piece was the towed M114A1 howitzer, the "one-five-five" or "penny-nickel-nickel." This 12,950 lb piece dates back to 1941 when it was adopted as the M1A1. It was towed by a 5-ton truck or lifted by a CH-54 Skycrane helicopter. Its 11-man crew could fire 12

Most 106mm M40A1 recoilless rifles were placed in storage or used only for base defense, but they were sometimes used for road clearance and convoy security. When placed in storage, the M151A1C jeeps were used for other purposes.

rounds in the first minute and maintain 1 rpm indefinitely. Despite its size it required only five minutes to emplace. The self-propelled version was the M109 on a full-tacked chassis and a fully rotating turret with a .50cal M2 machine gun on top. Both had a 14,600m (15,967 yd) range and their 95 lb HE round had a 360m (394 yd) casualty radius. Ammunition included HE, WP, burning smoke, improved conventional munition (ICM; 60 small bomblets called a "firecracker"), and illumination. The M108 and M109 had ten-man crews.[10]

Two self-propelled heavy artillery pieces were used in Vietnam. These were the 8in. or "eight-incher" M110 howitzer and the 175mm (6.8in.) "one-seven-five" M107 gun. The M110 howitzer was used by infantry division and corps artillery. With a range of 16,800m (10 mi), it was considered the most accurate artillery piece in the US inventory. Rounds could be "walked" onto a target as small as a bunker, but the proximity of friendly troops had to be considered owing to the wide fragmentation radius. On the other hand the M107 gun was used by corps artillery strictly as a long-range, area fire weapon and considered the least accurate piece. While a bit erratic, if properly serviced, it was reasonably accurate. Servicing included maintaining constant propellent temperatures, cleaning rounds, ensuring uniform ram depth for each round, maintaining precise fire direction center work, and calculating accurate meteorological data. Its 62,100m (38 mi) range had its uses. Its original barrel life was only 300 rounds, but later improved tubes were capable of enduring 700 then 1,200 rounds. Both weapons could be emplaced in 2–3 minutes and fired four to five rounds in the first three minutes. After that they fired about one round every two minutes. The only rounds were HE, 200 lb for the 8in. and 147 lb for the 175mm. Since the cradles were identical, an 8in. battery could retube all or some of its weapons in a few hours with 175mm barrels and vice

The 8in. M110 self-propelled howitzer was the most accurate artillery piece in the Army's inventory. The barrel could be switched with that of a 175mm gun, the most inaccurate artillery piece but valuable for its long range.

The 7.62mm M60 machine gun provided valuable fire support to rifle platoons. It was able to chop through the dense vegetation, and when long range was necessary, it was excellent.

10 See Osprey New Vanguard 86, M109 155mm Self-Propelled Howitzer, 1960-2005.

versa to fulfill different fire missions. This practice was first undertaken by Battery C, 7-15th Artillery in October 1967. Both were crewed by 12 men. The full-tracked chassis was unarmored and the guns unprotected by turrets. The same chassis was used for the M578 armored recovery vehicle.

Two air defense weapons provided valuable service in the ground role, being effective for base defense and delivering suppressive fire. The four-barrel M55 machine gun – the "quad-fifty" – was mounted in the cargo bed of a 2½-ton M35A1 gun truck. Each gun fired 550rpm. All four guns could be fired simultaneously, but usually two were fired alternatively to prevent overheating. There is a myth that the Hague Convention prohibits ".50cals" from being fired at personnel, but that it allows "enemy web gear to be fired at." There is no such restriction. The M42A1 "Duster" or "twin-forty" was an M41 light tank chassis mounting an open turret with two 40mm automatic cannons capable of 250rpm and crewed by four men. The VC called it the "Fire Dragon." Both Dusters and quad .50 gun trucks had an M60 and M79.

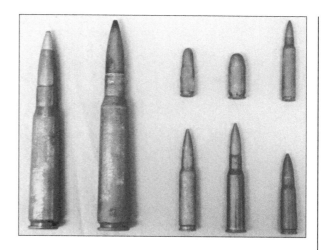

US and VC/NVA small arms ammunition. Left to right: the US .50cal and VC/NVA 12.7mm (aka the ".51cal") machine gun. (Both rounds are armor-piercing-incendiary.) Top row: VC/NVA 7.62mm pistol and submachine gun, US .45cal pistol, and US 5.56mm rifle. Bottom row: US 7.62mm NATO, VC/NVA 7.62mm rifle and machine gun, and VC/NVA 7.62mm AK assault rifle. The VC/NVA 12.7mm and three 7.62mm rounds are shown to demonstrate that they are not interchangeable with US ammunition, as is so often rumored.

Equipment

Vietnam's rough and varied terrain and harsh climate was a challenge to ground mobility, and a great deal of effort was expended developing ground vehicles. Regardless of imaginative developmental efforts, the reality was that there was not a lot that could be done to improve mobility through dense forests, in the mountains, across flooded rice paddies, and in swamps. Most wheeled vehicle traffic was restricted to highways, roads, the Central Highland plains, and dry paddies.

The ¼-ton 4x4 M151A1 utility truck (a Ford "jeep") was used as a command, reconnaissance, and liaison vehicle.[11] The M170 frontline ambulance was a variant. The ¾-ton M37B1 cargo truck was a 4x4 suitable for light utility work. The ambulance version was the M43B1. The 2½-ton 6x6 M35A2 and M135 cargo trucks (the "deuce and a half") were in the widest use, and the chassis was used for a wide range of support vehicles: 1,200-gal M49A2C fuel tanker, 1,000-gal M50A2 water tanker, M60 light wrecker, M109A2 shop van, M292A1 expandable CP van, and M342A2 dump truck. Larger versions were the 5-ton 6x6 M54 cargo truck and the M51 dump truck, 1,000-gal M61 water tanker, and M543 medium wrecker. Even heavier cargo trucks were the 10-ton 6x6 M125 and the M52 semitrailer tractor. An odd vehicle was the ½-ton M274-series utility platform truck, the "Mechanical Mule." It was used by airborne and airmobile units as a weapons and supplies carrier. It was the only vehicle that could carry more weight that it weighed itself. The ¼-ton M416, ¾-ton M101, and 1½-ton M103 two-wheeled cargo trailers were provided along with a wide range of specialized trailers including the 400-gal. (1,514-liter) M149 water trailer (the "water buffalo"). As an aside, the rated weight capacity of cargo trucks and trailers were for cross-country travel. On-road capacity was twice the rated capacity, e.g., a 2½-ton truck could carry 5 tons on-road. There were a great many specialized vehicles, including cargo carriers and engineer earthmoving and construction equipment. A key piece of engineer equipment was the Caterpillar D7E bulldozer fitted with a Rome plow blade, designed for splitting and felling large trees. Twenty-four "Rome plows" equipped each of the five engineer land-clearing companies, which leveled great swaths of jungle adjacent to roads and bases.

The crew of a 105mm M102 lightweight howitzer emplaces the gun in a reoccupied firebase. The "one-oh-five" was the principal fire support weapon.

11 The M151 is sometimes called the "MUTT" (Military Utility Tactical Truck). This was not an official designation nor was it generally used by soldiers, who instead referred to it as "one-five-one" or "jeep."

Command, control, communications, and intelligence

Command and control

Military Assistance Command, Vietnam (MACV), established in February 1962, was a joint command overseeing all US Army, Marines Corps, Air Force, and Navy forces in the country. MACV itself was subordinate to US Pacific Command. Army forces directly under MACV included: I and II FVV, XXIV Corps, 5th Special Forces Group, and all combat units. Various Free World Forces (Australian, Korean, and Thai) were also under MACV. US Army Vietnam (USARV, pronounced "USE-ar-vee"), created in July 1965, controlled various support and advisory organizations. Republic of Vietnam Armed Forces were not under MACV. There was no overall combined command, but they closely co-ordinated their activities.

The corps echelon of command in Vietnam was different from normal practices. South Vietnam was divided into four corps tactical zones, I–IV CTZ. These were ARVN organizational areas but were used by the United States for convenience. CTZs were divided into divisional tactical zones, but these were not used by the United States. On April 30, 1971, the CTZs were redesignated Military Regions (MR 1–4). With additional divisions and brigades arriving in Vietnam, two US corps-equivalent commands were established on March 15, 1966. I Field Force, Vietnam at Nha Trang was responsible for US forces in II CTZ. It had been formed as Field Force, Vietnam or Task Force ALPHA (Provisional) on August 1, 1965. XXX Corps Artillery Headquarters was serving as Task Force ALPHA's artillery headquarters and became I FFV Artillery. II FFV was established at Bien Hoa (later Long Bien) and controlled units in III CTZ. It was formed by redesignating XXII Corps Headquarters at Ft Hood, TX, in January 1966.

The "field force" concept was used rather than the traditional "army corps" to prevent confusion with the CTZs and numbered ARVN corps. The field force had additional responsibilities over a corps' normal role, which had only tactical control and combat support roles. The field force controlled US and certain allied units, fire support, aviation, combat support, logistics, and it provided advisory support to the ARVN. Additionally, the field force was a provisional command, and its vague designation made it appear less of a force escalation.

Army units in I CTZ were under the control of Marine Amphibious Force III. With increased deployment of Army units to the north to counter the 1968 Tet Offensive, MACV established MACV Forward as a temporary control headquarters on February 9. Provisional Corps, Vietnam was formed to replace it on March 10 at Phu Bai (moved to Da Nang in March 1970). This was consolidated with the new XXIV Corps Headquarters on August 18. XXIV Corps was subordinate to III MAF.

Divisions were the largest formations with a standard organization and were the primary command and control echelon for tactical units. A division controlled its maneuver battalions, artillery support, and combat service support units via three brigade, division artillery, and division support command headquarters as well as combat support units directly under division control. Flexibility was a key aspect of this organization, allowing any unit or element to be attached to another as required for the mission. Separate brigades functioned similarly. For example, units might be attached to a brigade, and the brigade commander could allocate elements of those units to his battalions and so on down the chain of command. This was called "operational control" (OPCON); it comprised the authority given to a commander to direct assigned forces, so that he could accomplish specific missions (the latter usually limited by function, time, or location). OPCON allowed a commander to deploy units concerned and to retain or assign tactical control of those units. It did not include the authority to assign separate employment of components of the units concerned. The commander was not burdened with the attached unit's administrative or logistic control, which remained the responsibility of the parent unit.

Battalions and higher-echelon units possessed a staff for planning, execution, and control of operations. The "principal staff" consisted of the S/G1 (personnel and administration), S/G2 (intelligence), S/G3 (operations and training), and S/G4 (logistics). Staff officers and their sections were identified by "S" (Staff) at battalion, regiment, group, and brigade levels and by "G" (General Staff) at division and higher. "J" (Joint Staff) designations were used at MACV level and by other joint service commands. A "G"staff was headed by the chief-of-staff. G-staff officers were designated, for example, deputy chief-of-staff for operations, the G3. The commander was also aided by an assistant commander (two in a division: one oversaw operations and the other logistics). Each staff officer had two to five assistant officers plus staff NCOs and enlisted men. There were also a number of "special staff" officers, with more being found at each ascending echelon. These might be dedicated specialist officers or the commander of supporting units, e.g., the commanders of the divisional artillery, aviation, engineer, adjacent general (admin) signal, and finance units. They might be physically represented on the staff by a liaison officer.

Maneuver battalion staffs had the CO (LTC), XO (MAJ), S1 (CPT), S2 (CPT), S3 (MAJ), S4 (CPT), communications officer (CPT), and motor officer (CPT). There was also an S3 Air (CPT), an assistant S3 in the battalion headquarters section. Support battalions usually lacked an S2, with his functions being taken over by the S3. These units usually had more special staff officers to manage their missions. Brigades and below had an executive officer as the second-in-command who oversaw and co-ordinated the staff much as a chief-of-staff.

US Army unit commander ranks	
Echelon	**Rank**
fire team	sergeant
squad	staff sergeant
section	NCO or officer[1]
platoon	lieutenant
detachment	lieutenant or captain
company/battery/troop	captain[2]
battalion/squadron	lieutenant colonel
regiment	colonel
group	colonel
brigade	colonel or brigadier general[3]
division	major general
field force/corps	major or lieutenant general

Notes:
1 A section could be part of a platoon or a separate section within a headquarter unit and could be commanded by an SSG, SFC, WO, or lieutenant.
2 Aviation company/troop COs were majors and platoon leaders were captains.
3 Divisional brigade COs were colonels and separate maneuver brigade COs were brigadier generals.

One of the reasons mortars were seldom taken to the field was the weight of their ammunition, about 9lb per round. Here a round in its black packing tube is fastened to a rifleman's rucksack.

Communications

The US Armed Forces established a complex and superb communications system throughout Vietnam. The division was supported by a robust signal battalion. The command operations company supported the headquarters and forward support element and operated headquarters message centers. The forward communications company provided signal center support to units in the division's forward area, supplemented the organic capabilities of units, and linked the brigade headquarters to other units. The signal support operations company provided communications for the division support command and other rear echelon elements, provided signal center support to rear units, and constructed radio relay and cable terminals. All three companies operated part of the communications system in the division's area. Separate brigades had a signal company attached; other signal support was provided by high-echelon signal units.

At any given echelon, a unit could talk to its higher headquarters and the other subunits within the unit on the "command net." There were also specialized nets to handle other radio traffic, which increased in number at each higher echelon.

At platoon level, the platoon leader, platoon sergeant, and the four squad leaders each carried an AN/PRC-6 walkie-talkie or AN/PRR-9 (helmet-mounted receiver) and AN/PRT-4 (harness-attached transmitter). All six individuals could speak to one another on the platoon net. Each platoon operated on its own net. In reality the squad radios were seldom used owing to weight and the constant need for batteries. The platoon RTO carried an AN/PRC-10, -25, or -77 backpack radio. The "Prick-25" was introduced in 1967–68 and became the mainstay platoon and company radio. This allowed the platoon leader to talk to the company CO and the other platoon leaders on the company command net. The weapons or mortar platoon, if employed, operated a platoon command net, linking each mortar and recoilless rifle. There was also a "fire direction net" with three mortar forward observers who accompanied the rifle platoons. They could talk directly to the mortar fire direction center. They could also talk to the supporting artillery unit, but they had to switch channels. Mechanized, tank, and armored cavalry units used similar nets, but every vehicle had a radio, while command vehicles had two or three radios on different nets.

On a conventional battlefield, the company CP had a vehicle-mounted AN/VRC-47 radio on the battalion command net, but, since vehicles were not used,

Radio-telephone operators (RTOs) of the company command group stand ready to board troop lift helicopters. They carry AN/PRC-25 radios festooned with M18 yellow smoke grenades. A UH-1B Huey gunship is buzzing the airstrip.

another backpack radio provided this link. The AN/VRC-47 was used in firebases and could be ground mounted. It could monitor two frequencies and transmit on one. The AN/VRC-46 could send and receive on one channel, and the AN/VRC-48 could transmit on one channel and monitor two channels. However, these had a restricted range when the companies were scattered afield. Jury-rigged "jungle antennas" might be suspended in a tree or contact could be maintained via helicopter relay radios. The different combat and support platoons under a battalion had their own internal nets and were also on the battalion command net. There was also a "battalion admin net" over which supply requests and "housekeeping" traffic were communicated. In firebases RC-292 pole antennas would be erected to provide longer-range communications.

Tanks, SP artillery, APCs, and other AFVs used the AN/VRC-12, -43, and -45, the equivalent of the AN/VRC-46, -47, and -48, but capable of intercom operation. The AN/VRC-53 was the vehicle-mounted version of the AN/PRC-25 while the AN/GRC-125 could be dismounted for manpack operation like the AN/PRC-25. All of these radios could net with one another.

US communications security was marginal, even though it was known that the NVA had the capability to monitor tactical traffic. However, there was so much tactical traffic that the NVA could only monitor some units with which they were engaged and only for short periods. US units used simple means of encrypting grid co-ordinates and had code words for certain items, supplies, individuals, and actions. Radio frequencies were changed infrequently, often only once a month, and many units retained the same call signs for their entire tour.

Field telephones were used in firebases to connect subunit headquarters, key facilities, artillery and mortar positions, and perimeter bunkers. The TA-312/PT and TA-1/PT were the standard phones, the latter being a small sound-power phone used at platoon level.

Ground-to-air communications was critical, both to identify friendly positions and enemy targets. Radio was the primary means, but friendly positions could be marked by colored smoke grenades, "pop-up" colored smoke signals, small marker panels, signal mirrors, and, at night, strobe lights, colored flashlights, pen flares, and pop-up colored flares. Colored smoke grenades were a common means of marking friendly positions, with yellow and purple smoke being the most common. Red signaled that a unit was in contact or it warned aircraft of enemy fire. Green was rarely used because it was difficult to detect against vegetation, although it was employed in dry season against yellowed vegetation.

Enemy positions were indicated by firing weapons such as 40mm grenades, mortars, and LAWs, including tracer fire at night. Describing the enemy's relation

Troops slip through a barbed wire fence surrounding a village occupied by the VC. Airmobile troops often conducted quick in-and-out strike missions, allowing them to travel light.

to terrain features identifiable from the air and by the compass azimuth, and determining distance from marked friendly positions, were common methods of indicating enemy locations. Once spotter aircraft and helicopter gunships could determine enemy positions, they would mark it with WP rockets.

Intelligence

Owing to the dense and rugged terrain, the elusive and dispersed enemy was not tied to fixed facilities or bases inside Vietnam. Furthermore, when the enemy used bases in favored sanctuaries in neighboring countries, US tactical intelligence was difficult to obtain and of uneven content.

A wide variety of means were used to collect tactical intelligence information. Within a division, this included:

- Aerial visual observation by the aviation battalion, air cavalry troop, brigade HHC, and DIVARTY HHB helicopters.
- Aerial radar and infrared surveillance by the aviation battalion (OV-1 Mohawks).
- Air Force forward air controllers (FAC).
- Radio intercept and locating by the ASA company.
- Artillery, rocket, and mortar locating by DIVARTY countermortar radar.
- Surveillance by infantry, armored cavalry, and artillery unit ground surveillance radar.
- Engineer terrain and route reconnaissance.
- Mounted reconnaissance by the armored cavalry troops.
- Deep ground reconnaissance by the LRP/Ranger company.
- Foot reconnaissance by maneuver battalion scout platoons and rifle company patrols.
- Detection assistance from scout dog, combat tracker teams, and Kit Carson scouts.
- Limited use of night vision observation devices and infrared searchlights.
- Constant vigilance.

There were also external intelligence sources that divisional units could exploit or employ: local Special Forces strike camps, Special Forces special reconnaissance projects, technical intelligence teams analyzing enemy equipment, meteorological units, Vietnamese Regional/Popular Forces[12], ARVN units, Vietnamese National Police Field Force, other Free World Military Forces, civilian informers, prisoner interrogations, and higher-unit intelligence resources, including those of other services, which were pushed down to tactical units in the form of periodic intelligence reports (PERINSUM), intelligence summaries (INSUM), and spot reports (SPOTREP). The division G2 Section and MI company would process, analyze, and dissimilate intelligence information to tactical units.

To the units on the ground it often seemed they were thrashing away in the dark at a crafty and agile phantom.

Infantrymen sweep across cultivated fields to search manure piles for hidden weapons. In the background, an M48A3 tank prowls down a road leading into the adjacent village.

12 RF/PF, or "Ruff-Puffs" – provincial and district militia for local security.

Combat status

Each of the seven divisions and various brigades committed to Vietnam had its own story of how it was activated, manned, deployed, and what its mission was once in-country. The units that follow are discussed in their order of deployment.

173rd Airborne Brigade (Separate)

The two-battalion "Sky Soldiers" brigade had been based on Okinawa as a Pacific regional contingency force since it was activated on March 26, 1963. Marine ground combat units had arrived in northern RVN on March 8, 1965. General Westmoreland requested the 173rd for temporary duty, and the deployment was approved on April 14. It was to be replaced by a 101st Airborne Division brigade. The 173rd was full strength and just about fully parachute qualified; about one man per squad was a "leg." Arriving on May 7 by airlift and sea, one battalion was deployed to secure Vung Tau where other Army units were disembarking. The other secured the developing base at Bien Hoa, northwest of Saigon. While US forces were authorized to conduct offensive operations on April 6, the 173rd did not begin preparations for such until early June after the 1st Bn, Royal Australian Regt and 161st Field Battery, Royal New Zealand Artillery were attached from May 5, 1965–May 16, 1966. After practicing airmobile operations, it executed its first combat action on June 27. On August 5 the brigade was taken off TDY orders and assigned to Vietnam. In late 1966 it fought numerous battles in War Zone C. What became known as the "Herd" grew to the largest brigade in the Army with the addition of 4-503rd Infantry in June 1966 and the 3-503rd in October 1967. The 1-50th Infantry (Mech), relieved from the 2nd ArmdDiv at Ft Hood, TX, arrived in Vietnam in September 1967 and was attached to the 173rd from May 1968–September 1969. The 3-506th Infantry of the 101st AbnDiv was attached from December 1969 to April 1970. From its arrival upto October 1967, the 173rd

173rd Airborne Brigade (Separate)
1st–4th Bn (Abn), 503rd Infantry
3rd Bn (105mm) (Abn), 319th Artillery
Co D (Tank) (Abn), 16th Armor[1]
Trp E (Armd), 17th Cavalry
Co N (Ranger), 75th Infantry[2]
173rd Support Bn (Abn)
173rd Engineer Co (Cbt) (Abn)
534th Signal Co (Abn)[3]
335th Aviation Co (Ambl)
76th Infantry Det (Cbt Tracker)
172nd MI Det
404th ASA Det
39th Infantry Platoon (Scout Dog)
Notes:
1 Deactivated August 25, 1968.
2 Replaced 74th Infantry Det (LRP) February 1, 1969.
3 Replaced 173rd Signal Co (Prov) December 20, 1968.

The 173rd Airborne Brigade (Separate), the "Sky Soldiers," became known as the "Herd."

The 101st Airborne Division. The "Screaming Eagles" were also known as the "Puking Buzzards." The division retained its Airborne tab for traditional reasons when it was reorganized as an airmobile division and lost its jump status.

was based at Bien Hoa. It moved to An Khe in II CTZ in October 1967 and the next month was involved in the bitter battle for Dak To. It remained there until relocated to Bong Song in northern II CTZ in May 1969 where it remained until departing. Most of the brigade's actions in 1968 and beyond were fought in Binh Dinh and Binh Thuan Provinces. The 173rd conducted the only large-scale US airborne operation in Vietnam, when, on February 22, 1967, 845 troops of Brigade HHC elements, 2-503rd Infantry and Btry A, 3-319th Artillery jumped onto Drop Zone Red outside Katum in support of an airmobile operation involving eight US and allied battalions. Its later operations were mainly line-of-communications security. The 173rd departed Vietnam on August 25, 1971, for Ft Campbell, KY, where it was inactivated on January 14, 1972.

1st Brigade, 101st Airborne Division

This brigade was selected to relieve the 173rd and began arriving by sealift at Cam Ranh Bay on July 29, 1965. Home-based at Ft Campbell, KY, it was fully parachute qualified, with troops being drawn from other divisional units. It was moved to Bien Hoa and Vung Tau where it remained until September, then moved back to Cam Ranh Bay. The brigade continued to operate in II CTZ, being based at Ma Ca (November 1965), Phan Rang (December 1965), Duk Pho (June 1967), and then split between Phan Rang and Duk Pho (July 1967). It operated throughout II CTZ and conducted some operations in southern I CTZ. It was attached to Task Force OREGON in May 1967. On November 23, 1967, the 3-506th Infantry was attached from the parent division to provide a fourth maneuver battalion. The battalion would spend much of the war attached to other units such as the 173rd, Task Force South and I FFV. The 1st Bde, 101st AbnDiv relocated back to Bien Hoa in November 1967 to rejoin its parent division. Both the 173rd and 1st Bde, 101st AbnDiv were maintained at full parachute-qualified strength at the expense of later deploying airborne units to provide airborne reaction forces. Two brigades were necessary, in the event one was committed to ground combat. The brigade returned home in January 1972.

1st Brigade, 101st Airborne Division
1st & 2nd Bn (Abn), 327th Infantry
2nd Bn (Abn), 502nd Infantry
2nd Bn (105mm) (Abn), 320th Artillery
101st Support Bn (Prov)
Trp A, 2nd Sqdn (Armd) (Abn), 17th Cavalry
Co A, 326th Engineer Bn (Cbt) (Abn)
Co D, 326th Medical Bn (Abn)
Co B, 501st Signal Bn (Abn)
20th Chemical Det
181st MI Det
406th ASA Det
42nd Infantry Plat (Scout Dog)

1st Cavalry Division (Airmobile)

In February 1963 the cadres for the 11th Air Assault Div and 10th Air Transport Bde were activated as test units at Ft Benning, GA. An entirely new doctrine was to be developed for which little guidance or experience existed. Extensive testing and exercises took place to develop airmobile tactics, and the division grew. On June 15, 1965, it was redesignated the 1st CavDiv (Airmobile) – the "First Team." At the time the 1st CavDiv was serving in Korea as an infantry

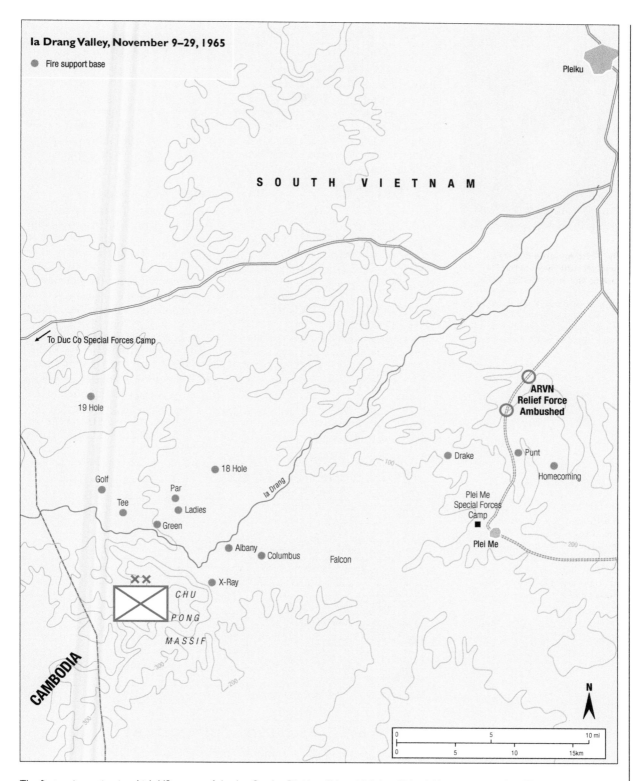

Ia Drang Valley, November 9–29, 1965

● Fire support base

Pleiku

S O U T H   V I E T N A M

← To Duc Co Special Forces Camp

● 19 Hole

ARVN
Relief Force
Ambushed

● Drake

● Punt

● 18 Hole

● Homecoming

● Golf

● Par

Ia Drang

Plei Me
Special Forces
Camp

● Tee

● Ladies

● Green

■

● Albany

Plei Me

● Columbus

Falcon

● X-Ray

CHU

PONG

MASSIF

CAMBODIA

N

0		5		10 mi
0	5	10	15km	

The first major action in which US troops of the 1st Cavalry Division (Airmobile) faced North Vietnamese regulars. The division employed its extensive helicopter assets to establish fire support bases and deployed troop units over a large area to search out and engage the enemy. The firebases were mutually supportive. The various infantry battalions on the ground would be supported from multiple bases.

The insignia of the 1st Cavalry Division (Airmobile), the "First Team," also known simply as the "Cav," was about three times as large as other divisions' insignias and was known as the "blanket patch." Its 1st Brigade initially wore a gold-on-black Airborne tab.

1st Cavalry Division (Airmobile)

1st–3rd Bde, 1st CavDiv (Ambl)
1st & 2nd Bn (Ambl), 5th Cavalry
1st, 2nd & 3rd Bn (Ambl), 7th Cavalry
1st[1] & 2nd[1] Bn (Ambl), 8th Cavalry
1st[1] & 2nd Bn (Ambl), 12th Cavalry
DIVARTY, 1st CavDiv
2nd Bn (105mm)(Ambl), 19th Artillery[1]
2nd Bn (105mm)(Aerial Rocket), 20th Artillery
1st Bn (105mm)(Ambl), 21st Artillery
1st Bn (155mm), 30th Artillery[2]
1st Bn (105mm)(Ambl), 77th Artillery
Battery E (Aviation), 82nd Artillery
11th Aviation Group
227th & 229th Aviation Bn (Assault Helicopter)
228th Aviation Bn (Assault Support Helicopter)
11th Aviation Co (General Support)
11th Pathfinder Co (Prov)
17th Aviation Co (Fixed Wing Transport)[3]
478th Aviation Co (Heavy Helicopter)[3]
1st Aviation Det (ACH-47)(Prov)[3]
53rd Aviation Det (Field Evacuation)(Prov)[3]
DISCOM, 1st CavDiv (Ambl)
1st Personnel Service Bn (Prov)[4]
15th Medical Bn (Ambl)
15th Quartermaster Supply Bn (Ambl)
15th Transportation Bn (Aircraft Maint)(Ambl)
27th Ordnance Maintenance Bn (Ambl)
15th Administrative Co (Ambl)
1st Sqdn (Air), 9th Cavalry
8th Engineer Bn (Cbt)(Ambl)
13th Signal Bn (Ambl)
545th MP Co (Ambl)
191st MI Co
Co H (Ranger), 75th Infantry[5]
371st ASA Co
14th Military History Det
41st & 42nd Public Information Det
16th & 184th Chemical Plat
25th, 34th, & 37th Infantry Plat (Scout Dog)
62nd Infantry Plat (Cbt Tracker)
FIRST TEAM Academy

Notes:
1. Also Airborne until November 1966.
2. Assigned June 1, 1968. Previously attached.
3. Attached.
4. Existed January 26, 1968 to July 1, 1969.
5. Co E (LRP), 52nd Infantry prior to February 1, 1969.

division.[13] Its colors were swapped with the 2nd InfDiv's at Ft Benning as it was thought the designation would effectively describe the division capabilities as "air cavalry." While sometimes referred to as the "1st Air Cavalry Division," this is incorrect. By absorbing what had been the 2nd InfDiv, the "1st Cav" was to be fully manned and equipped by the end of July as its mobility was judged ideal over Vietnam's rugged terrain. At the time the division had only 9,500 of its required 15,900 men. Half of the assigned troops were due for discharge or were ineligible for overseas deployment. Among them were hundreds of experienced aircrew and maintenance personnel. Additional air crewmen were arriving who had not yet flown the new helicopters.

The division's 1st Bde and its supporting elements were parachute qualified. As troops were rotated after a year, this capability dwindled, and the Army made no effort to replace them with paratroopers. They lost their airborne status in November 1967.

An advance party of "Skysoldiers" was airlifted to Vietnam in August to prepare a base of operations near the An Khe Special Forces Camp in the Central Highlands. At the end of July the division began its sea movement, and the division arrived September 11 through late October. The 1st Cav deployed with only eight battalions but received 5th Bn, 7th Cavalry on August 20, 1966. It was also augmented by additional small aviation units. The division would maintain An Khe as its main base until April 1969. During that time it would forward base at Bong Song (January 1968), Hue (February 1968), Phong Dien (April 1968), Quang Tri (May 1968), Phong Dien again (October 1968), and Phuoc Vinh (April 1969). It commenced offensive airmobile operations in the enemy-controlled Ia Drang Valley to interdict NVA units infiltrating from Cambodia, resulting in major battles between US and NVA troops. Through 1966 until the Tet Offensive the division fought in II CTZ, but in February–March 1968 it was pressed into the vicious battle for Hue. After a stint in northern I CTZ into late 1968 where it took part in the relief of Khe Sanh, the division deployed south to War Zone D in III CTZ in November to help protect Saigon from increasing NVA efforts. It also sent units into IV CTZ, making the division the only one to operate in all four corps areas. It was the main force committed to the May–June 1970 Cambodia invasion to destroy NVA bases.

The division troops and 1st Bde departed on April 29, 1971, followed by the 2nd Bde on March 26. The 3rd Bde remained as a separate brigade (discussed later). The 1st ArmdDiv at Ft Hood, TX, was reflagged as the 1st CavDiv and became a test unit for the "triple-capability" (TRICAP) concept that combined airmobile, mechanized, and tank units. TRICAP proved to be impractical, and it was converted to an armored division in 1974–75.

On September 1, 1970, the 1st CavDiv formed a unique unit, the 9th Air Cavalry Bde (Prov) and recognized it on December 5. Its mission was to conduct air and ground reconnaissance missions over a large area in III CTZ along the Cambodian border. The effective brigade was disbanded on February 15, 1971, in preparation for the division's withdrawal.

9th Air Cavalry Brigade (Provisional)
1st Sqdn (Air), 9th Cavalry
3rd Sqdn (Air), 17th Cavalry
Trp E (Armd), 17th Cavalry
Co H (Ranger), 75th Infantry
62nd Infantry Plat (Cbt Tracker)

13 It is rumored that the 1st CavDiv once lost its colors in an unspecified war and that its colors would not be returned to the States. This is a myth.

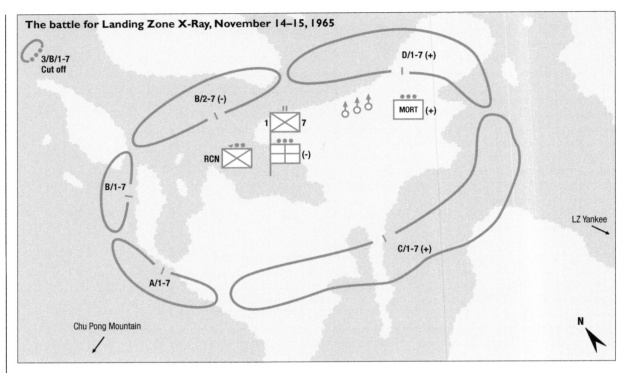

The battle for Landing Zone X-Ray, November 14–15, 1965

3/B/1-7 Cut off

B/2-7 (-)

D/1-7 (+)

MORT (+)

1 7

RCN

(-)

B/1-7

LZ Yankee

C/1-7 (+)

A/1-7

Chu Pong Mountain

N

The reinforced 1st Battalion, 7th Cavalry of the 1st CavDiv (Ambl) fought a bitter two-day battle on LZ X-Ray against three NVA regiments. Some 450 Skytroopers fought off 3,000 enemy troops. This example is typical of a hasty battalion defensive perimeter.

The 1st Infantry Division was known as the "Big Red One," or the "Big Dead One" by the more fatalistic. This nickname meant so much to the troops that many refused to wear the subdued patch with a black "1."

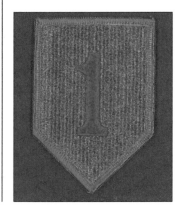

1st Infantry Division

Based at Ft Riley, KS, the "Big Red One" was alerted to deploy a brigade as rapidly as possible to Vietnam. The division had only seven infantry battalions, and the nonmechanized 1-2nd and 2-2nd Infantry were reassigned from the 5th InfDiv (Mech), replacing its two tank battalions. The division's two mechanized battalions (1-26th and 1-28th) were converted to straight leg. The division was not allowed to take a tank battalion, as was desired by the commander. The opinion was that Vietnam's terrain and the conflict's nature were ill suited for mechanized operations. Constant requests for its tank battalion were rejected, but in 1967 and 1968 two infantry battalions were converted to mechanized (2-2nd, 1-16th). The 2nd Bde (2-16th, 1-18th and 2-18th Infantry, and 1-7th Artillery) arrived July 11, 1965, ahead of the division. It was based at Bien Hoa and soon engaged in combat operations. The division headquarters arrived in October, immediately followed by the 3rd and 1st Brigades. In February 1966 the division moved to Di An between Binh Hoa and Saigon. It would operate in III CTZ throughout the war alongside the 25th InfDiv. The division was spilt between Di An and Lai Khe, north of Saigon, in February 1967, then concentrated at Lai Khe in October, and finally relocated to Di An in November 1969 where it remained until April 15, 1970, and retuned on paper to the States. In 1971 the 24th InfDiv (Mech) at Ft Riley and a brigade in Germany were reflagged as the 1st InfDiv (Mech).

1st Infantry Division
1st–3rd Bde, 1st InfDiv
1st & 2nd (Mech)[1] Bn, 2nd Infantry
1st (Mech)[2] & 2nd Bn, 16th Infantry

Continues on following page

1st & 2nd Bn, 18th Infantry
1st Bn, 26th Infantry
1st & 2nd Bn, 28th Infantry
DIVARTY, 1st InfDiv
1st Bn (105mm), 5th Artillery
8th Bn (155mm/8in.), 6th Artillery
1st Bn (105mm), 7th Artillery
2nd Bn (105mm), 33rd Artillery
DISCOM, 1st InfDiv
1st Medical Bn
1st QM Supply & Motor Transportation Bn
701st Ordnance Maint Bn
1st Administrative Co
1st Sqdn (Armd), 4th Cavalry
1st Engineer Bn (Cbt)
1st Aviation Bn
121st Signal Bn
1st MP Co
1st MI Co
337th ASA Co
Co I (Ranger), 75th Infantry[3]
17th Military History Det
43rd & 44th Public Information Det
242nd Chemical Det
35th & 41st Infantry Plat (Scout Dog)
61st Infantry Plat (Cbt Tracker)
262nd Chemical Plat
1st InfDiv Replacement Training Center

Notes:
1 Converted to mechanized January 1967.
2 Converted to mechanized October 1968.
3 Co F (LRP), 52nd Infantry prior to February 1, 1969.

The 25th Infantry Division was the "Tropic Lightning," having been raised in Hawaii and having fought in the Pacific in World War II.

25th Infantry Division

The "Tropic Lightning Division" was based at Schofield Barracks, HI, when it was alerted for deployment to Vietnam. It was the main Pacific reserve force. It had been sending volunteer helicopter door gunners to Vietnam since early 1963. The 25th was preparing for a training and security mission to Thailand; however, it remained at home station until a new unit could be raised on Hawaii in the form of the 11th InfBde, to fill the viod for Pacific response. The 3rd Bde deployed by air, departing December 23, 1965, to arrive at Pleiku in the Central Highlands. The 2nd Bde arrived by ship at Vung Tau on January 20, 1966, and was flown to Cu Chi northwest of Saigon. To fill out the understrength division, two battalions, 4-9th and 4-23rd Infantry, were reassigned from the 171st and 172nd InfBdes in Alaska, and the 1-69th Armor arrived in January and February. The 2-14th Infantry remaining in Hawaii had been stripped to fill the other battalions. Refilled with recruits, it arrived in April. The division headquarters arrived on March

28, 1966, followed by the 1st Bde on April 28. Through great effort the division had deployed five months earlier than scheduled. Cu Chi remained the division's base throughout its tour. The 3rd Bde, however, operated separately from Pleiku. On August 1, 1967, the 25th exchanged its 3rd Bde with the 4th InfDiv's 3rd Bde, which had been operating in III CTZ. Brigade designations and shoulder patches changed, but the battalions retained their designations. Oddly enough these brigades' tank battalions, 1-69th and 2-34th Armor, had been assigned to the 25th and 4th InfDivs, respectively, but had been deployed to other areas upon arrival and were now back with their original divisions. Most of its operations were conducted in northwest III CTZ, but in 1968 it conducted operations in southern III CTZ and in Saigon during the Tet counteroffensive. It soon returned to its main TAOR, and elements participated in the April–May 1970 Cambodian invasion.

The division departed on December 8, 1970, returning to Hawaii and was reduced to zero strength except for the 1st Bde. The 4th Bde (which had been activated in Hawaii and never deployed) was reflagged as the 1st Bde. The 2nd Bde remained as a separate brigade (discussed later). In 1972 the 25th was reactivated in Hawaii.

25th Infantry Division		
1st–3rd Bde, 25th InfDiv		
1st Bn (Mech), 5th Infantry		
4th Bn, 9th Infantry		
2nd Bn, 14th Infantry		
4th Bn (Mech), 23rd Infantry[1]		
1st & 2nd Bn, 27th Infantry		
3rd Bde, 25th InfDiv[2]	3rd Bde, 4th InfDiv[3]	
	1st Bn, 14th Infantry	2nd Bn, 12th Infantry
	1st & 2nd Bn, 35th Infantry	2nd (Mech) & 3rd Bn, 22nd Infantry
	2nd Bn, 34th Armor	1st Bn, 69th Armor
DIVARTY, 25th InfDiv		
1st Bn (105mm), 8th Artillery		
7th Bn (105mm), 11th Artillery		
3rd Bn (155mm/8in.), 13th Artillery		
2nd Bn (105mm), 9th Artillery[2]; 2nd Bn (105mm), 77th Artillery[3]		
DISCOM, 25th InfDiv		
1st–3rd Support Bn (Prov)[4]		
25th Medical Bn		
25th QM Supply & Motor Transportation Bn		
725th Ordnance Maint Bn		
25th Administrative Co		
3rd Sqdn (Armd), 4th Cavalry		
25th Aviation Bn		
65th Engineer Bn (Cbt)		

Continues on following page

125th Signal Bn
25th MP Co
25th MI Co
372nd ASA Co
Co F (Ranger), 75th Infantry[5]
9th Chemical Det
15th & 20th Public Information Det
18th Military History Det
38th, 46th, & 60th Infantry Platoon (Scout Dog)
66th Infantry Platoon (Combat Tracker)
Lightning Replacement Training School

Notes:
1 Converted to mechanized January 1967.
2 Units transferred to 4th InfDiv August 1, 1967.
3 Units transferred from 4th InfDiv August 1, 1967.
4 Formed June 1, 1966, from DISCOM medical, supply & transport, and maintenance companies to support brigades.
5 Co F (LRP), 50th Infantry prior to February 1, 1969.

196th Infantry Brigade (Light) (Separate)

Activated on September 10, 1965, at Ft Devens, MA, as the first ROAD infantry brigade, the 196th planned to take over the 1st Bde, 82nd AbnDiv's Dominican Republic peacekeeping mission. It was filled with raw recruits and cadres from the 5th InfDiv (Mech). With inadequate training facilities, it struggled to be ready for its Caribbean mission in July 1966. In early May, however, it was decided the brigade was not needed in the Dominican Republic, and it was offered to Westmoreland. Notified on June 24, the brigade had to be partly rebuilt owing to the necessity to transfer soldiers ineligible for combat deployment, exchange M14 rifles and qualify on the M16A1, and draw newer radios and other equipment. The brigade was airlifted to Vietnam on August 26 and based at Tay Ninh in northwest III CTZ where the 1st Bde, 25th InfDiv assisted in its train-up. In April 1967 it was moved to I CTZ, attached to Task Force OREGON, and based at Chu Lai. On September 25 it was made a component of the AMERICAL Div. Moves were frequent, with the brigade being based at Tam Ky (November 1967), Phong Dien (April 1968), Hoi An (June 1968), Chu Lai (July 1968), and finally Da Nang (April 1971) for port security with the departure of the 3rd Marine Div. From August 1971, after the AMERICAL Div was inactivated, it operated again as a separate brigade with the addition of other units.

The 196th Infantry Brigade (Light) (Separate) bore the motto "Ahead of the Rest." The insignia depicted the slow match used by fusiliers to fire their matchlock muskets.

196th Infantry Brigade (Light) (Separate)
2nd Bn (Lt), 1st Infantry
3rd Bn (Lt), 21st Infantry
4th Bn (Lt), 31st Infantry
1st Bn, 46th Infantry[1]
3rd Bn (105mm), 82nd Artillery
8th Support Bn[2]
196th Support Bn (Prov)[1]

Continues on following page

Trp F (Air), 8th Cavalry[1]
Trp F (Armd), 17th Cavalry
175th Engineer Co (Cbt)
196th Signal Co (Prov)
587th Signal Company[1,3]
10th Public Information Det
27th Chemical Det
408th ASA Det
544th MP Det
569th MI Det
48th Infantry Plat (Scout Dog)
Cbt Tracker Team 10/64th Infantry Det (Cbt Tracker)
Team 2, 635th MI Det

Notes:
1 Units attached from August 1971–June 1972 after AMERICAL Div inactivated, and the
   brigade operated separately.
2 Inactivated February 15, 1969 (previously disestablished September 1967).
3 Replaced 196th Signal Co (Prov) August 1971.

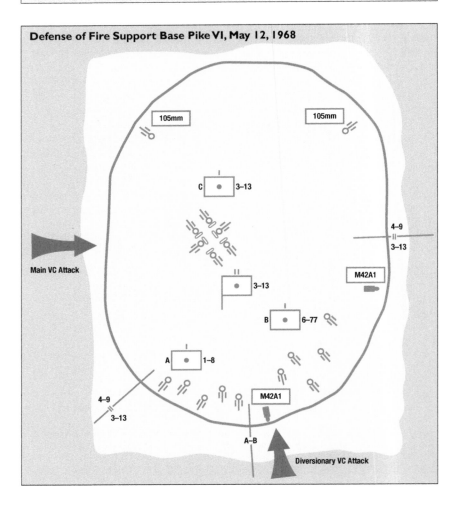

Defense of Fire Support Base Pike VI, May 12, 1968

An infantry battalion and three howitzer batteries defended this firebase southwest of Saigon. The 3-13th Artillery defended the south and southeast end of the perimeter with attached batteries A/1-8th Artillery and B/6-77th Artillery, with five of their six 155mm howitzers on the perimeter for direct fire with beehive rounds. They each positioned one howitzer on the north end of the perimeter for direct fire. C/3-13th positioned its 155mm SP howitzers in the center for all-round fire and in direct support to other units. Two M42A1 Dusters were positioned at the south end and on the east side. A diversionary attack was launched by the VC from the south, and this managed to damage a Duster. The main attack struck from the west. With the help of another 155mm battery to the northeast, the attack was defeated after a 2½-hour fight. US losses were five dead and 30 wounded. Some 110 VC bodies were counted.

The brigade departed on June 29, 1972, to be inactivated at Oakland, CA on the 30th. It left behind the 3-21st Infantry, supported by Btry G (105mm) (Prov), 29th Field Artillery, which remained until August 23, becoming the last infantry battalion to leave.

11th Armored Cavalry Regiment

Regardless of the earlier perceived need for no armor, the 11th ACR was requested to open a main line of communications through III CTZ. Westmoreland preferred a mechanized brigade. He was told that the 199th InfBde, undergoing preparation for Vietnam, could be converted to mech, necessitating the deactivation of the 11th ACR, and that the 199th's deployment would be delayed. He opted for the 11th ACR, but its tanks were replaced by ACAVs. The "Blackhorse Regiment" was almost 2,000 men understrength when alerted in March 1966. Training areas were scarce in the Washington, DC, area, and the unit was forced to train at smaller scattered bases. In August the unit was flown to California and its equipment sent by rail. Departing by ship it arrived at Vung Tau September 7–19, 1966, with 4,200 troops; its attached units formed 549 of the total. It spent a brief time at Bien Hoa preparing for operations and then moved to Long Binh where it remained until March 1967. It then moved to Xuan Loc, operating from there until it moved to Lai Khe in February 1969. It almost immediately relocated to Long Giao until September, then on to Bien Hoa in October. In July 1970 it made its final move to Di An. Besides operating as a brigade-equivalent force, its squadrons were occasionally detached to divisions in III CTZ, especially the 1st CavDiv during the Cambodian invasion.

The insignia of the 11th Armored Cavalry Regiment, "Blackhorse Regiment," bore the red and white of cavalry *guidons*.

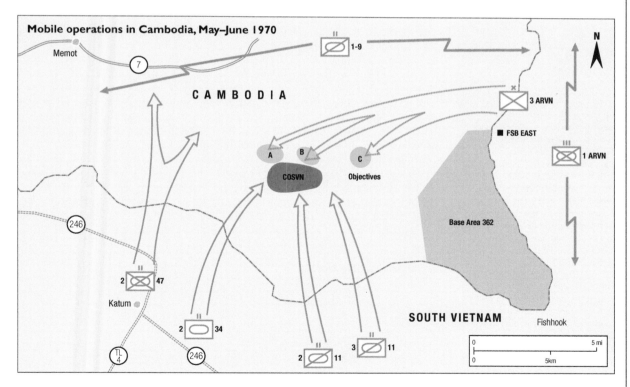

The efforts to neutralize sanctuaries inside Cambodia involved both US and ARVN forces and demonstrated the ability for armor/mechanized forces to operate in dense terrain. From the east the 3rd ARVN Airborne Brigade was air assaulted onto its objectives – enemy base areas. The 1st CavDiv's 1-9th Air Cavalry screened to the north, while the 1st ARVN Armored Cavalry Regiment (battalion sized) screened the eastern border. The 2nd and 3rd squadrons of the 11th ACR thrust north, aiming at the Central Office of South Vietnam (COSVN) headquarters area, along with 2-34th Armor, while the 2-47th Infantry (Mech) moved in to block escape to the west.

On March 5, 1971, most of the regiment departed. The 2/11th remained until inactivated on April 2, 1972, and the Air Cav Trp left in March. The 14th ACR at Fulda, Germany, was reflagged as the 11th ACR on May 17, 1972.

11th Armored Cavalry Regiment
1st–3rd Sqdn, 11th ACR
Air Cavalry Trp, 11th ACR
37th Medical Co
919th Engineer Co (Cbt)
Co B(-), 720th MP Bn
17th Public Information Det
28th Military History Det
33d Chemical Det
75th Infantry Det (Cbt Tracker)
124th Avionics Det
202nd & 541st MI Det
390th Transportation Det
409th ASA Det
7th Automatic Data Processing Unit
46th Infantry Plat (Scout Dog)

4th Infantry Division

The 4th Infantry Division, the "Ivey Division," was also known as the "Poison Ivey."

The "Ivey Division" at Ft Lewis, WA, was alerted in April 1966 for deployment. A division was desperately needed in the Central Highlands. The 2nd Bde was the first to deploy, arriving by sea on August 10, 1966, and was flown to Pleiku. The rest of the division arrived in early October to join the 2nd Bde, except the 3rd Bde, which was deployed to III CTZ to operate with the 25th InfDiv. It was transferred to the 25th InfDiv, swapping it for the 4th InfDiv's 3rd Bde, which had been serving with Task Force OREGON in I CTZ. The division remained at Pleiku until it moved to Ah Khe in April 1970. It spent March 1968 at Dak To. In 1970 it participated in the Cambodia invasion. All of its service was in central II CTZ.

It departed Vietnam on December 7, 1970, although its 3rd Bde departed on April 15 and was inactivated at Ft Lewis. The rest of the division returned to Ft Lewis where it was rejoined by its old 3rd Bde from the 25th InfDiv, sent from Hawaii and inactivated. The 1-22nd Infantry remained in Vietnam as a separate battalion until January 30, 1972, at Tuy Hoa. In 1971 the assets of the 5th InfDiv (Mech) at Ft Carson were reflagged as the 4th InfDiv (Mech).

4th Infantry Division		
1st–3rd Bde, 4th InfDiv		
1st, 2nd (Mech)[1], & 3rd Bn, 8th Infantry		
4th Bn, 9th Infantry		
1st & 3rd Bn, 12th Infantry		
1st Bn, 22nd Infantry		
1st & 2nd Bn, 27th Infantry		
3rd Bde, 4th InfDiv[2]		3rd Bde, 25th InfDiv[3]
	2nd Bn, 12th Infantry	1st Bn, 14th Infantry
	2nd (Mech) & 3rd Bn,	1st & 2nd Bn, 35th

	22nd Infantry¹	Infantry
	1st Bn, 69th Armor	2nd Bn, 34th Armor
DIVARTY, 4th InfDiv		
2nd Bn (155mm/8in.), 16th Artillery		
6th Bn (105mm), 29th Artillery		
4th Bn (105mm), 42nd Artillery		
2nd Bn (105mm), 77th Artillery;[2] 2nd Bn (105mm), 9th Artillery[3]		
DISCOM, 4th InfDiv		
4th Medical Bn		
4th QM Supply & Motor Transportation Bn		
704th Ordnance Maint Bn		
4th Administrative Co		
1st Sqdn (Armd), 10th Cavalry		
4th Aviation Bn		
4th Engineer Bn (Cbt)		
124th Signal Bn		
4th MP Co		
4th MI Co		
374th ASA Co		
Co K (Ranger), 75th Infantry[4]		
43rd Chemical Det		
14th Public Information Det		
29th Military History Det		
33rd, 50th, & 60th Infantry Platoon (Scout Dog)		
63rd & 64th Infantry Platoon (Combat Tracker)		
4th InfDiv Replacement Training Committee		

Notes:
1 Converted to Mechanized May 1967.
2 Units transferred to 25th InfDiv August 1, 1967.
3 Units transferred from 25th InfDiv August 1, 1967.
4 Co E (LRP), 20th Infantry; replaced by Co E (LRP), 58th Infantry, January 10, 1968, and prior to February 1, 1969.

199th Infantry Brigade (Light) (Separate)

The 199th was raised at Ft Benning, GA, specifically for Vietnam duty, on June 1, 1966. Its formation, equipping, and training were extremely rushed. Advanced training was conducted in Mississippi with units still much understrength. The "Redcatchers" were flown to California and shipped to arrive at Vung Tau beginning on December 10 and were based at Long Bien. Seven days later the unit executed its first airmobile assault. In April 1967 it moved to Bien Hoa and then back to Long Bien in July. In March 1968 it moved to Gao Ho Nai and then again to Long Bien in July. Its primary mission was the defense of the Saigon area, and it conducted operations all around the capital. Elements fought inside Saigon during the Tet Offensive. Being on the edge of the Mekong Delta, it conducted some riverine operations supported by the 1099th Transportation Company (Medium Boat).

The only light infantry brigade to remain separate for its entire tour, the 199th departed Vietnam on October 11, 1970, and was inactivated at Ft Benning on October 15.

The 199th Infantry Brigade (Light) (Separate) carried the motto "Light, Swift, and Accurate" but was commonly known as the "Redcatchers," owing to the red flame in the insignia's center, reminiscent of the catcher's baseball mitt.

199th Infantry Brigade (Light) (Separate)
2nd Bn (Lt), 3rd Infantry
3rd Bn (Lt), 7th Infantry
4th & 5th Bn (Lt), 12th Infantry
2nd Bn (105mm), 40th Artillery
7th Support Bn
87th Engineer Co (Cbt)
313th Signal Co
Trp D (Armd), 17th Cavalry
Co M (Ranger), 75th Infantry[1]
40th Public Information Det
44th Military History Det
76th Infantry Det (Cbt Tracker)
503rd Chemical Det
856th ASA Det
49th Infantry Platoon (Scout Dog)
152nd MP Platoon
Note:
1 Co F (LRP), 51st Infantry until December 26, 1968. M-75th attached February 1, 1969.

9th Infantry Division

The "Old Reliables" were the first division to be raised specifically for Vietnam duty. Approved in January 1966 it was activated on February 1 at Ft Riley, KS. Training cadres, equipment, and ammunition insufficiencies delayed effective training until April. A full division staff was not assembled until June. Troops destined for the 5th InfDiv at Ft Carson were diverted to the 9th. Alerted for deployment its training was cut short so that it would arrive in the Mekong

A reinforced rifle company of the 9th InfDiv securing two 105mm howitzer batteries fought off a concerted VC night attack supported by heavy machine guns, recoilless rifle, and mortar and rifle grenade fire. The listening posts on the east side of the canal were cut off, but most of the reconnaissance platoon made it into the main perimeter. Despite six dead and 98 wounded, the Americans held, although two howitzers were destroyed in the 1½-hour battle. The VC may have lost up to 200 dead.

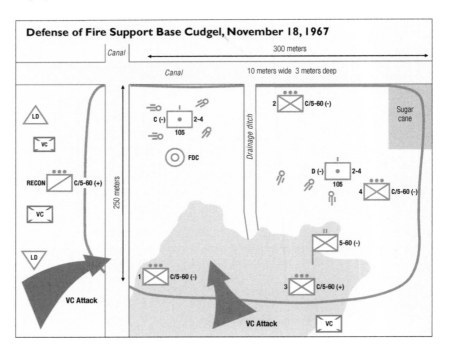

Defense of Fire Support Base Cudgel, November 18, 1967

Delta at the beginning of the dry season. Just before deployment, the 2-27th Infantry was reorganized as a mech battalion, giving it two, with one battalion in the 1st and 3rd Bdes. The division began arriving at Vung Tau on December 16, 1966, and was sent to Bear Cat in CTZ IV. The 1st and 2nd Bdes arrived in January. The 2nd Bde was detailed to the Mobile Riverine Force alongside the Navy's River Assault Flotilla One (Task Force 117) and operated in that manner until departing. In August 1968 the division relocated to Dong Tam. In April 1968 6/31st Infantry was sent from Ft Lewis. The 5/60th Infantry (Mech) lost its tracks in September 1968 to the 1/16th Infantry, 1st InfDiv. The 9th operated in IV CTZ throughout its tour.

The first division to be withdrawn, it was sent home in increments. The 1st Bde departed Vietnam on August 12, 1969, followed by the Division

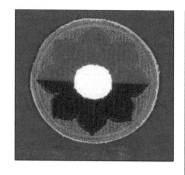

The 9th Infantry Division's troops were known as the "Old Reliables."

9th Infantry Division
1st–3rd Bde, 9th InfDiv
6th Bn, 31st Infantry
2nd, 3rd, & 4th Bn, 39th Infantry
2nd (Mech), 3rd[1], & 4th[1] Bn, 47th Infantry
2nd, 3rd[1], & 5th[2] Bn, 60th Infantry
DIVARTY, 9th InfDiv
2nd Bn (105mm), 4th Artillery
1st Bn (105mm), 11th Artillery
3rd Bn (105mm), 34th Artillery[1]
1st Bn (155mm/5-in), 84th Artillery
DISCOM, 9th InfDiv
9th Medical Bn
9th QM Supply & Motor Transportation Bn
709th Ordnance Maint Bn
9th Administrative Co
3rd Sqdn (Armd), 5th Cavalry
9th Aviation Bn
9th Signal Bn
15th Engineer Bn (Cbt)[3]
9th MP Co
9th MI Co
335th ASA Co
Co E (Ranger), 75th Infantry[4]
18th & 19th Public Information Det
19th & 47th Military History Det
39th Chemical Det
43rd & 45th Infantry Plat (Scout Dog)
65th Infantry Plat (Cbt Tracker)
Reliable Academy
Notes:
1 Assigned to 2nd Bde for riverine operations.
2 Mechanized prior to September 1968.
3 Co C supported 2nd Bde riverine operations.
4 Co E (LRP), 50th Infantry prior to February 1, 1969.

Headquarters on August 27 going to Hawaii. The 2nd Bde had left on July 28. The 3rd Bde remained as a separate brigade (discussed later). The entire division was inactivated in Hawaii, but reactivated in 1972 at Ft Lewis.

Task Force OREGON

TF OREGON was in effect a provisional division formed in I CTZ on April 12, 1967, to counter increasing enemy activity in southern corps area, as the 1st and 3rd Marine Divisions were tied down in the north. Based at Cu Lai, it was composed of brigades from the 25th InfDiv and 101st AbnDiv plus a separate brigade. These brigades were dispatched from areas where the enemy threat was then minimal. The division support command was provided by the 15th Support Bde, previously intended to manage direct and general support units; other support units were acquired in-country. There was no division artillery headquarters. Under the control of Marine Amphibious Force III, the task force conducted aggressive operations from May through September 1967. In August the 3rd Bde, 25th InfDiv was redesignated 3rd Bde, 4th InfDiv without changing its subordinate unit designations. The 1st Bde, 101st AbnDiv left the Task Force and was replaced by the 3rd Bde, 1st CavDiv.

In September the AMERICAL Div was activated, taking over the area of operations and much of TF OREGON's assets, including the 196th InfBde. The other two brigades were released back to their parent commands. TF OREGON was disbanded on September 22, 1967.

Task Force OREGON
3rd Bde, 25th InfDiv[1]
1st Bn, 14th Infantry
1st & 2nd Bn, 35th Infantry
2nd Bn (105mm), 9th Artillery
1st Bde, 101st AbnDiv
1st & 2nd Bn (Abn), 327th Infantry
2nd Bn (Abn), 502nd Infantry
2nd Bn (105mm) (Abn), 320th Artillery
101st Support Bn (Prov)
Trp A, 2nd Sqdn (Armd) (Abn), 17th Cavalry
196th InfBde (Lt) (Sep)
2nd Bn (Lt), 1st Infantry
3rd Bn (Lt), 21st Infantry
4th Bn (Lt), 31st Infantry
3rd Bn (105mm), 82nd Artillery
8th Support Bn
Trp F (Armd), 17th Cavalry
15th Support Bde
94th Supply & Service Bn (Direct Support)
188th Maint Bn (Direct Support)
3rd Bn (155mm), 16th Artillery
3rd Bn (175mm), 18th Artillery
1st Sqdn (Armd), 1st Cavalry

Continues on following page

2nd Sqdn, 11th Armd Cavalry Regt
Trp C, 1st Sqdn (Air), 9th Cavalry
15th Aviation Bn (Cbt)
39th Engineer Bn (Cbt)
509th Signal Bn (Support)

Notes:
Only battalion-sized units and cavalry troops belonging to the brigades are shown. See the appropriate entry for other brigade units.
1 Redesignated 3rd Bde, 4th InfDiv August 1967.

AMERICAL Division (23rd Infantry Division)

The AMERICAL Div was the first division raised overseas since 1942, and like its World War II predecessor it was assembled using separate in-country units. Also like its predecessor the AMERICAL Div would be fighting alongside the Marines. Much was made of the unit being the only named division, but it was actually designated the 23rd InfDiv, a designation that was largely ignored. Its abbreviated designation was AMCAL. Activated on September 25, 1967, at Cau Lai in I CTZ where it remained, the in-country 196thInfBde was assigned. The 15th Support Bde became the DISCOM on December 8, 1967. The engineer battalion was provided four combat companies and a float bridge company. The brigade support battalions were inactivated and their companies absorbed into the new support units. The 198th InfBde arrived in October and was assigned to be followed by the 11th InfBde in December. Being assigned its own aviation group, the division possessed nearly all the capabilities of an airmobile division, especially important owing to the size of its TAOR. On February 14, 1969, the three brigades' battalions were assigned to the division and could now be switched between brigades as necessary. On October 15, 1969, the division's subordinate units were reorganized under the standard infantry division TO&E, reducing its service units by 750 troops. However, the brigades retained their original designations, and the separate cavalry troops were retained rather than consolidated into a squadron. While operating mainly in southern I CTZ, it conducted operations in every province in the corps area.

The AMERICAL's support units were inactivated in-country through November 1971, leaving the 196th InfBde behind as a separate unit. The division was reduced to zero strength, and a color party was sent to Ft Lewis, where the division was inactivated on November 29.

AMERICAL Division (23rd InfDiv)
11th, 196th, & 198th Infantry Bde (Lt) (Sep)
2nd[2] & 3rd[1] Bn, 1st Infantry
4th Bn, 3rd Infantry[1]
1st Bn, 6th Infantry[3]
1st Bn, 20th Infantry[1]
3rd[2] & 4th[1] Bn, 21st Infantry
4th Bn, 31st Infantry[2]
1st & 5th Bn, 46th Infantry[3]
1st Bn, 52nd Infantry[3]

Continues on following page

The AMERICAL Division, or officially, the 23rd Infantry Division, displayed the Southern Cross.

	Organized from:
DIVARTY, AMERICAL Div	
6th Bn (105mm), 11th Artillery[1]	
1st Bn (105mm), 14th Artillery[3]	
1st Bn (155mm/8in.), 82nd Artillery[4]	
3rd Bn (105mm), 82nd Artillery[2]	Organized from:
DISCOM, AMERICAL Div	15th Support Bde[6]
23rd Medical Bn	brigade medical companies
23rd QM Supply & Motor Transportation Bn	94th Supply & Service Bn
723rd Ordnance Maint Bn	188th Maint Bn (Direct Support)
23rd Administrative Co	Co A, 6th Support Bn
16th Aviation Group (Cbt)	
14th Aviation Bn (Cbt)	
123rd Aviation Bn (Airmobile)	161st Aviation Co (Ambl, Lt)
212th Aviation Bn (Cbt)	
26th Engineer Bn (Cbt); 6th[1], 175th[2], 554th, 555th[3] Engr Co & Co B, 39th Engr Bn	
523rd Signal Bn	509th Signal Bn
23nd MP Co	
635th MI Co	
328th ASA Co	
335th Transportation Co (Aircraft Direct Support)	
Trp E (Armd), 1st Cavalry[1]	
Trp F (Air), 8th Cavalry[5]	
Trp F (Armd)[2] & Trp H (Armd)[3], 17th Cavalry	
Co G (Ranger), 75th Infantry[7]	
3rd Military History Det	
10th[2] & 31st[1] Public Information Det	
27th[2], 87th[3], & 90th[1] Chemical Det	
48th[2], 57th[3], & 59th[1] Infantry Plat (Scout Dog)	
63rd & 557th Infantry Plat (Cbt Tracker)	
Chu Lai Defense Command	
AMERICAL Combat Center (Prov)	

Notes:

1 Originally with 11th InfBde.

2 Originally with 196th InfBde.

3 Originally with 198th InfBde.

4 Assigned July 31, 1968. Previously general support was provided by attached 3rd Bn (155mm), 16th Artillery.

5 Attached to 123rd Aviation Bn.

6 Brigade maintenance and supply companies became forward support companies.

7 Co E (LRP), 51st Inf organized December 2, 1968, from Det A (LRP), itself formed from 196th InfBde LRP Det and LRP personnel from 11th and 198th InfBde. Replaced by G-75 Infantry, February 1, 1968.

198th Infantry Brigade (Light) (Separate)

The "Brave and Bold" brigade was activated on May 10, 1967 at Ft Hood, TX, and slated as the Practice Nine Barrier Brigade to man the planned and ill-conceived "McNamara Line" (aka Muscle Shoals and Igloo White), stretching along the 17th Parallel Demilitarized Zone. Fortunately the barrier system was never constructed, and the 198th was slated for the AMERICAL Div. The brigade was sent to California and shipped to Vietnam, arriving at Da Nang on October 21, 1967. On October 26, it was assigned to the AMERICAL Div. It was based at Duk Pho until moved to Chu Lai in December. The unit departed Vietnam on October 13, 1971 after being reduced to zero strength, and was inactivated at Ft Lewis on November 30.

The 198th Infantry Brigade (Light) (Separate) carried the motto "Brave and Bold." The Roman shield was the standard insignia shape for separate brigades.

198th Infantry Brigade (Light) (Separate)
1st Bn (Lt), 6th Infantry
1st & 5th Bn (Lt), 46th Infantry
1st Bn (Lt), 52nd Infantry
1st Bn (105mm), 14th Artillery
9th Support Bn[1]
Trp H (Armd), 17th Cavalry
555th Engineer Co (Cbt)
47th Military History Det
87th Chemical Det
601st ASA Det
635th MI Det
47th Signal Plat
Note:
1 Inactivated February 15, 1969 (previously disestablished after arrival in Vietnam).

101st Airborne Division (Airmobile)

The 101st AbnDiv was based at Ft Campbell, KY, and its 1st Bde had been in Vietnam since July 1965. Once an all-airborne unit and part of the Strategic Army Corps' response force, the "Screaming Eagles" possessed few paratroopers due to maintaining the 1st Bde in fully parachute-qualified status. Alerted in August 1966, the rest of the division was to deploy to Vietnam in February 1967, filling with parachute-qualified troops from the 82nd AbnDiv. Training and equipage constraints delayed it until November. Some 10,000 troops were flown to Vietnam on December 18–19 to set up base at Bien Hoa. It was the largest airlift of a combat force into a combat zone to date. The 1st Bde was still in II CTZ with Task Force OREGON. While maintaining its main base at Bien Hoa (elements would remain there into 1969), the bulk of the division deployed north to I CTZ in March 1968 and saw action at Hue. Its main northern base was at Phu Bai. In August the 3rd Bde was sent to III CTZ to beef up the 25th InfDiv and returned north in September.

In January 1968 the Army had conducted a study of its ability to produce trained paratroopers and the number of airborne units it could maintain. The 82nd AbnDiv, the strategic reserve, had priority for paratroopers. However, Special Forces, LRP units, and airborne battalions and companies in Europe, Panama, and Alaska as well as in Vietnam, needed paratroopers

Landing Zone (LZ) Sally was a 101st AbnDiv (Ambl) base northwest of Hue. Such bases provided a home for headquarters, service, and support units. Long-range artillery units and aviation units operated from these bases as well. Note the airstrip and helipads in the upper right.

101st Airborne Division (Airmobile)
1st–3rd Bde, 101st AbnDiv (Ambl)
3rd Bn, 187th Infantry
1st & 2nd Bn, 327th Infantry
1st & 2nd Bn, 501st Infantry
1st & 2nd Bn, 502nd Infantry
1st, 2nd, & 3rd Bn, 506th Infantry
DIVARTY, 101st AbnDiv
2nd Bn (155mm), 11th Artillery[1]
4th Bn (Aerial Rocket), 77th Artillery[2]
2nd Bn (105mm), 319th Artillery
2nd Bn (105mm), 320th Artillery
1st Bn (105mm), 321st Artillery
Battery A (Aviation), 337th Artillery[2]
101st Aviation Group[3]
101st Aviation Bn
158th & 159th Aviation Bn (Assault Helicopter)[2]
163rd Aviation Co (General Support)[2]
478th Aviation Co (Heavy Helicopter)
DISCOM, 1st CavDiv (Ambl)
5th Transportation Bn (Aircraft Maint)(Ambl)[2]
326th Medical Bn (Ambl)
426th Quartermaster Supply Bn (Ambl)
801st Ordnance Maintenance Bn (Ambl)
101st Administrative Co (Ambl)
2nd Sqdn (Air), 17th Cavalry[4]
326th Engineer Bn (Cbt)(Ambl)
501st Signal Bn (Ambl)
101st MP Co (Ambl)
101st MI Co
Co L (Ranger), 75th Infantry[5]
265th ASA Co
20th & 36th Chemical Det
22nd Military History Det
25th, 34th, & 45th Public Information Det
10th Chemical Plat
42nd, 47th, & 58th Infantry Plat (Scout Dog)
557th Infantry Plat (Cbt Tracker)
Screaming Eagle Replacement Training School (SERTS)

Notes:
1 Assigned June 10, 1968.
2 Assigned December 1968 or earlier, during conversion.
3 160th Aviation Group from July 1, 1968–June 25, 1969, then 101st.
4 Converted from armored cavalry to air cavalry, December 1968–June 1969.
5 Co F (LRP), 58th Infantry prior to February 1, 1969.

too. The report said that it would be difficult to maintain only the 173rd Abn Bde in Vietnam with sufficient paratroopers, much less the 1st Bde, 101st. The entire 101st would be taken off jump status and converted to an airmobile division. This process was ordered on June 28, 1968. The division was designated as 101st AbnDiv (Airmobile) on August 26. Conversion to airmobile had been considered prior to its deployment to Vietnam, but insufficient numbers of helicopters were available.

The division was based at Bien Hoa in III CTZ. This would remain its main base even when committed far to the north. In early 1968 it operated in northern areas as well as in Hue during the Tet Offensive. Late 1968 saw brigades operating in I, II, and III CTZ. In September 1968 the division was concentrated in I CTZ where it remained. Bases were established at Phu Bai, Gia Le, and Hue. The 101st took part in the last major US offensive, JEFFERSON GREEN, from September 1970 to October 1971. The division's aviation elements supported the January–April 1971 ARVN incursion into Laos. The 3rd Bde departed on December 21, 1971, the 1st Bde on January 19, 1972, along with the DIVARTY and DISCOM, and then the 2nd Bde on February 14. The division returned to Ft Campbell at 20 percent strength, the last division to leave Vietnam. Its 3rd Bde was placed on airborne status, carrying on the traditions, not the lineage, of the 173rd AbnBde. The division was redesignated the 101st AbnDiv (Air Assault) on October 4, 1974 (the 3rd Bde had lost its airborne status the previous February).

3rd Brigade, 82nd Airborne Division

The 3rd Bde, 82nd AbnDiv was alerted for Vietnam in January 1968, and it was airborne en route to Chu Lai on February 13. The division's 2nd Bde was stripped to fill out the 3rd with qualified paratroopers. (The 82nd was part of the strategic reserve, and while it was considered for deployment to Vietnam, it remained in the States.) Upon arrival it was discovered that the majority was ineligible for Vietnam deployment owing to having been deployed within the past two years or for other reasons. Of the 3,650 troops, 2,513 were immediately sent home, and the brigade was filled with nonairborne replacements. These men would have been sent to other units where they were desperately needed, so in effect the brigade's rushed deployment was detrimental. It remained an "airborne" brigade in name only. (The 82nd raised a 4th Bde at Ft Bragg to replace the 3rd, but it remained understrength.) The 3rd Bde was first based at Phu Bai and attached to the 1st CavDiv at Hue. In September it moved to Phu Loi outside Saigon under the control of the Capital Military Assistance Command where it operated until returning home. It was the shortest-serving separate brigade in Vietnam and the first to return home. The "Golden Brigade" departed on December 11, 1969, and rejoined the "All Americans" when the 4th Bde was reflagged as the 3rd.

The 3rd Brigade, 82nd Airborne Division was known as the "All Americans," but it was said the "AA" meant "almost airborne," owing to the sometimes low percentage of assigned paratroopers.

3rd Brigade, 82nd Airborne Division
1st & 2nd Bn (Abn), 505th Infantry
1st Bn (Abn), 508th Infantry
2nd Bn (105mm) (Abn), 321st Artillery
82nd Support Bn
Trp B, 1st Sqdn (Armd), 17th Cavalry
Co O (Ranger), 75th Infantry
Co C, 307th Engr Bn (Cbt) (Abn)
52nd Chemical Det
408th ASA Det
518th MI Det

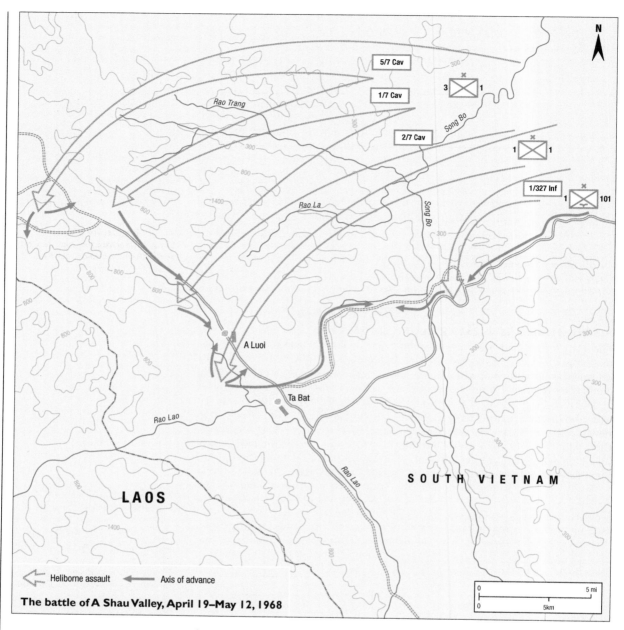

The battle of A Shau Valley, April 19–May 12, 1968

Legend:
Heliborne assault — Axis of advance

Map labels: 5/7 Cav, 1/7 Cav, 2/7 Cav, 1/327 Inf, Rao Trang, Rao La, Rao Lao, Song Bo, A Luoi, Ta Bat, LAOS, SOUTH VIETNAM, N

The A Shau Valley in west-central I CTZ on the Laotian border was a longtime VC/NVA stronghold. Frequent efforts were made to destroy enemy staging bases in the region. Seven 1st CavDiv and 101st AbnDiv battalions were air assaulted into the valley while two other 101st battalions were moved by ground on the south side of the AO.

1st Brigade, 5th Infantry Division (Mechanized)

The only mechanized brigade to serve in Vietnam was stationed at Ft Carson, CO, when alerted for deployment in March 1968. It was reorganized as a separate brigade, and besides one tank and one mech infantry battalion, it included a standard infantry battalion to conduct airmobile operations. The Kansas National Guard's 69th InfBde (Separate) was mobilized to replace the 1st Bde at Ft Carson. The 1st Bde was moved by rail to California and then by ship to arrive in Vietnam on July 22, 1968. It would be a month before it was combat ready owing to its rushed deployment. It operated mostly in northern I CTZ, supporting the Marines operating out of Quang Tri. The "Red Devils" departed Vietnam in mid-August 1971, and the brigade was inactivated to Ft Carson on August 22, as the 5th InfDiv was reflagged as the 4th.

1st Brigade, 5th Infantry Division (Mechanized)
1st Bn, 11th Infantry
1st Bn (Mech), 61st Infantry
1st Bn (Tank), 77th Armor
5th Bn (155mm SP), 4th Artillery
75th Support Bn
Co A, 7th Engineer Bn (Cbt)
Co P (Ranger), 75th Infantry[1]
298th Signal Co (Brigade)
48th Public Affairs Det
77th Infantry Det (Cbt Tracker)
407th ASA Det
517th MI Det
77th Infantry Platoon (Scout Dog)
Note:
1 79th Infantry Det (LRP) prior to February 1, 1969.

The 1st Brigade, 5th Infantry Division (Mechanized) was known as the "Red Diamonds" or "Red Devils."

11th Infantry Brigade (Light)

The 11th InfBde had been activated on July 1, 1966, at Schofield Barracks to reestablish a Pacific response force in the absence of the 25th InfDiv. The brigade was not fully manned or fully equipped when ordered to Vietnam as an emergency response. Some 1,300 of its troops were ineligible for deployment and had to be replaced. The Hawaii National Guard's 29th InfBde (Separate) was mobilized to replace it. When it arrived on December 19, 1967, many of its newly assigned troops had not participated in unit training. It was assigned to the AMERICAL Div upon arrival and based at Duk Pho. It remained there until July 1971 when it moved to The Loi. The brigade folded in Vietnam and was inactivated at Ft Lewis with the AMERICAL Div on November 29, 1971.

11th Infantry Brigade (Light)
3rd Bn (Lt), 1st Infantry
4th Bn (Lt), 3rd Infantry[1]
1st Bn (Lt), 20th Infantry
4th Bn (Lt), 21st Infantry[2]
6th Bn (105mm), 11th Artillery
6th Support Bn[3]
Trp E (Armd), 1st Cavalry
6th Engineer Co (Cbt)
31st Public Information Det
70th Infantry Det (LRP)
90th Chemical Det
327th Aviation Det
59th Infantry Platoon (Scout Dog)
Notes:
1 Reattached to 198th InfBde, August 1971.
2 Assigned April 14, 1968.
3 Inactivated February 15, 1969 (previously disestablished September 1967).

The 11th Infantry Brigade (Light) was known as the "Jungle Warriors." "(Separate)" was not appended to its designation as it was assigned directly to the AMERICAL Division.

A rifle squad crosses a rocky stream in the hills. Extra canteens and rucksacks filled with three to five days' rations are evident.

3rd Brigade, 9th Infantry Division

The 9th InfDiv departed Vietnam in September 1969, but the 3rd Bde remained at Tan An in southern III CTZ under the 25th InfDiv. It conducted operations in that area as well as some in IV CTZ. As a separate brigade, it was detached from the 9th on July 26, 1969. The "Go Devils" returned to the States on October 11, 1970, and the unit was inactivated at Ft Lewis.

3rd Brigade, 9th Infantry Division
6th Bn, 31st Infantry
2nd Bn (Mech), 47th Infantry
2nd & 5th Bn, 60th Infantry
2nd Bn (105mm), 4th Artillery
99th Support Bn
Trp D (Air), 3rd Sqdn, 5th Cavalry
Co E (Ranger), 75th Infantry
56th Signal Co
571st Engineer Co (Cbt)
39th Cavalry Platoon (Air Cushion Vehicle)

2nd Brigade, 25th Infantry Division

The 2nd Bde was detached from the 25th InfDiv on November 8, 1970, and the rest of the division departed the following month. Located at Long Binh and Xuan Loc, it operated under II FFV control around Saigon until departing on April 30, 1971. It was reduced to zero strength in Hawaii.

2nd Brigade, 25th Infantry Division
1st Bn (Mech), 5th Infantry
2nd Bn, 12th Infantry
3rd Bn, 22nd Infantry
1st Bn, 27th Infantry
1st Bn (105mm), 8th Artillery
Trp F (Air), 4th Cavalry
Co F (Ranger), 75th Infantry

A heavily burdened rifleman steps off a Huey skid. He carries a lightweight rucksack with an aluminum frame. This allowed him to carry more easily the gear necessary for extended operations.

3rd Brigade, 1st Cavalry Division (Airmobile)

Based at Bien Hoa, the 3rd Bde remained as a separate brigade from April 30, 1971, when the division departed. Operating under II FFV control, it served as a reaction force for the Saigon area. The brigade departed on June 26, 1972, and when the 4th Bde (organized in its absence) was reflagged the 3rd Bde at Ft Hood. Task Force GARRY OWEN was formed in Vietnam using remaining 3d Brigade assets.

The 155mm M114A1 howitzer, the "one-five-five," was a valuable fire support weapon. Each division had a battalion of 18, and there were eight nondivisional battalions.

3rd Brigade, 1st Cavalry Division (Airmobile)
2nd Bn (Ambl), 5th Cavalry
1st Bn (Ambl), 7th Cavalry
2nd Bn (Ambl), 8th Cavalry
1st Bn (Ambl), 12th Cavalry
1st Bn (105mm) (Ambl), 21st Field Artillery
Btry F (105mm) (Prov), 26th Field Artillery
Btry F (Aviation), 77th Field Artillery
215th Support Bn
229th Aviation Bn (Assault Helicopter)
362nd Aviation Co (Assault Support Helicopter)
Btry F (Aerial Rocket), 79th Field Artillery
Trp F (Air)(Prov), 9th Cavalry
Co H (Ranger), 75th Infantry
501st Engineer Co (Cbt)
14th Military History Det
26th Chemical Det

Task Force GARRY OWEN

This could be called the last brigade in Vietnam. Consisting only of a reinforced infantry battalion and a single artillery battery, it did possess significant aviation assets, which were engaged in the battle of An Loc north of Saigon. It was formed on June 26, 1972, and remained until August 22, protecting the Bien Hoa–Saigon–Long Binh area.

Task Force GARRY OWEN
1st Bn (Ambl), 7th Cavalry
Co C, 2nd Bn (Ambl), 5th Cavalry
Btry F (105mm) (Prov), 26th Field Artillery
Btry F (Aerial Rocket), 79th Field Artillery
Co H (Ranger), 75th Infantry
501st Engineer Co (Cbt)
229th Aviation Bn (Assault Helicopter)
362nd Aviation Co (Assault Support Helicopter)
Trp F (Air) (Prov), 9th Cav[1]

Note:
1 Unofficially known as Trp H (Air), 16th Cavalry.

Lessons learned

M113A1 armored cavalry assault vehicles (ACAV) of the 11th Armored Cavalry Regiment are accompanied by an M48A3 tank. Armored vehicles were vulnerable to RPGs and recoilless rifles, but more were lost to mines or got stuck in the mud than anything else.

As Vietnam was a small-unit war, countless lessons were learned at this level. Operations and movement on rugged terrain and in limited visibility, patrolling, ambushes and counterambush, employment techniques of all types of weapons, close combat using AFVs, directing supporting fires, communications, and airmobile operations were just some of the areas in which valuable lessons were learned and areas in which new techniques were developed that carried over into postwar tactics. Especially valuable advances were made in uniform and individual equipment design and materials, ammunition packaging, field rations, and medical procedures.

Organizationally it was learned that units could fight with leaner manpower. Unit reorganizations in the 1970s saw more streamlined structuring. Aviation units saw the greatest change. They were made smaller and more agile, making them easier to control, although many more were fielded. The Army had undeniably mastered the value of air mobility and its many uses.

There was a downside though. America lost this war. It makes no difference who or what the cause was. The Army had been turned into a hollow force, as NCOs left in large numbers – as did combat-experienced younger troops who would have filled the void. Drug, race, and morale problems counteracted unit *esprit de corps*, traditions, and cohesion, processes that were intensified by both low opinions of the army held both by the public and by the army itself. The experience left a sour taste in the mouths of too many Army leaders. Consequently many of the valuable lessons learned were ignored if they were too closely related to the Vietnam conflict. What followed was a rapid return to conventional doctrine and tactics, as the Soviet threat was "rediscovered," and the Army reoriented itself for the defense of Western Europe. Even though the many contingency operations conducted through the 1990s saw insurgents, guerrillas, and terrorists as the opposition, many in the Army still resisted training exercises involving such opponents, preferring instead heavy conventional forces. Indeed, many of the lessons learned in Vietnam at such a high cost could be applied to the conflicts in which the US Army finds itself engaged today.

Chronology

1955–63

March 1955   First US military advisers arrive in Vietnam.

July 21, 1955   Vietnam divided at the 17th Parallel as the French withdraw.

January 1959   North Vietnam issues resolution that changes its "political struggle" in South Vietnam to an "armed struggle."

May 1959   North Vietnam begins major improvements on the Ho Chi Minh Trail to supply its struggle in the south.

December 1960   National Liberation Front (Viet Cong) formed.

February 6, 1962   Military Assistance Command, Vietnam (MACV) formed to control all US armed forces in RVN.

November 22, 1963 President John F. Kennedy is assassinated. Lyndon B. Johnson becomes president.

1964

June 20   Gen William Westmoreland assumes command of MACV.

August 2–4   Destroyers USS *Maddox* and *C. Turner Joy* allegedly attacked by North Vietnamese torpedo boats in the Gulf of Tonkin.

August 7   US Congress passes Gulf of Tonkin Resolution to counter North Vietnamese aggression.

November 3   Johnson elected president.

1965

February 7   VC attacks US installations in Pleiku. Johnson authorizes air attacks on North Vietnam, commencing on February 24.

March 8   First US Marine ground combat troops arrive in RVN.

April 6   US ground troops authorized to conduct offensive operations.

May 7   First US Army conventional ground combat troops arrive in RVN, the 173rd AbnBde (Sep).

July 30   US Army, Vietnam (USARV) activated to control Army logistical and support forces.

September 11   1st CavDiv (Ambl) arrives in RVN.

October 2   1st InfDiv arrives in RVN.

1966

March 15   I and II FFVs activated.

March 28   25th InfDiv arrives in RVN.

August 26   196th InfBde (Lt) (Sep) arrives in RVN.

September 8   11th ACR arrives in RVN.

September 25   4th InfDiv arrives in RVN.

December 10   199th InfBde (Lt) (Sep) arrives in RVN.

December 16   9th InfDiv arrives in RVN.

1967

April 12   Task Force OREGON formed.

September 22   Task Force OREGON disbanded.

September 25   AMERICAL Div activated in RVN.

October 21   198th InfBde (Lt) (Sep) arrives in RVN.

November 19   101st AbnDiv arrives in RVN.

December   Antiwar protests increase in the United States.

December 19   11th InfBde (Lt) arrives in RVN.

1968

January 30   VC and NVA initiate Tet Offensive, which ends February 26.

January 31   Battle for Hue. Completed February 25.

March 31   US Government announces de-escalation of its war effort and halts bombing of North Vietnam.

May 12   Peace talks begin in Paris.

July 1	Gen Creighton Abrams assumes command of MACV, and Gen Westmoreland becomes Chief of Staff of the Army.
July 25	1st Bde, 5th InfDiv (Mech) arrives in RVN.
August 15	XXIV Corps activated.
November 6	Richard M. Nixon elected president.

1969

June 8	US initiates Vietnamization program to completely turn the war effort over to RVN forces.
August 27	9th InfDiv (-) departs RVN.
October 11	3rd Bde, 9th InfDiv departs RVN.
December 11	3rd Bde, 82nd AbnDiv departs RVN.

1970

April 15	1st InfDiv departs RVN.
April 29	US offensive operations into Cambodia to neutralize NVA/VC sanctuaries. Operation completed June 30.
October 11	199th InfBde (Lt) (Sep) departs RVN.
November 7	Nixon is re-elected.
December 7	4th InfDiv departs RVN.
December 8	25th InfDiv (-) departs RVN.

1971

April 29, 1971	1st CavDiv (Ambl) (-) departs RVN.
April 30	2nd Bde, 25th InfDiv departs RVN. I FFV inactivated.
May 2	II FFV inactivated.
June 28	Last 1st Marines elements depart RVN.
August 25	173rd AbnBde (Sep) departs RVN.
August 27	1st Bde, 5th InfDiv (Mech) departs RVN.
November 12	US forces cease offensive operations but could support Vietnamese forces.
November 13	11th and 198th InfBdes depart RVN.
November 29	AMERICAL Div departs RVN.

1972

March 10	101st AbnDiv (Ambl) departs RVN.
May 15	USARV inactivated.
June 26	3rd Bde, 1st CavDiv (Ambl) departs RVN.
June 29	196th InfBde departs RVN.
June 30	XXIV Corps inactivated.
August 23	3rd Battalion, 21st Infantry is the last combat unit to depart RVN.

1973

January 15	US announces the halt of all offensive ground action.
January 27	Ceasefire agreement is signed in Paris. US conscription ceases.
March 29	Final US troops are withdrawn from RVN. MACV is disbanded.

1974

August 9	Nixon resigns presidency and is replaced by Gerald Ford.

1975

April 29	US embassy in Saigon evacuated.
April 30	Saigon falls to NVA forces.

1976

June 2	Socialist Republic of Vietnam established by uniting North and South Vietnam.

Bibliography

Bertle, Andrew J. *US Army Counterinsurgency and Contingency Operations Doctrine, 1942–1976*. Vietnam Studies series. (Washington, DC: Department of the Army, 2006.)

Cash, John A.; Albright, John; and Sandstrum, Allan W. *Seven Fire Fights in Vietnam*. Vietnam Studies series. (Washington, DC: Department of the Army, 1985.)

Hay, John H., Jr. *Tactical and Materiel Innovations*. Vietnam Studies series. (Washington, DC: Department of the Army, 1989.)

Kelly, Michael. P. *Where We Were in Vietnam: A Comprehensive Guide to the Firebases, Military Installations and Naval Vessels of the Vietnam War, 1945–1975*. (Central Point, OR: Hellgate Press, 2002.)

Ott, David E. *Field Artillery, 1954–1973*. Vietnam Studies series. (Washington, DC: Department of the Army, 1975.)

Stanton, Shelby. *The Rise and Fall of an American Army: U.S. Ground Forces in Vietnam, 1965–1973*. (Novato, CA: Presidio Press, 1985.)

—— *Vietnam Order of Battle: A Complete Illustrated Reference to U.S. Army Combat and Support Forces in Vietnam 1961–1973*. (Mechanicsburg, PA: Stackpole Books, 2003.)

Starry, Donn R. *Mounted Combat in Vietnam*. Vietnam Studies series. (Washington, DC: Department of the Army, 1989.)

Tolson, John J. *Airmobility, 1961–1971*. Vietnam Studies series. (Washington, DC: Department of the Army, 1973.)

The Vietnam Studies series books can be found online at the US Army Center for Military History Web site:

http://www.army.mil/cmh-pg/online/Bookshelves/books-era.htm

Abbreviations

Abn	Airborne	HQ	Headquarters
ACAV	armored cavalry assault vehicle	Inf	Infantry
ACR	Armored Cavalry Regiment	LRP	Long-Range Patrol
AFV	armored fighting vehicle	Lt	Light
Ambl	Airmobile	MACV	Military Assistance Command, Vietnam
AO	Area of Operations	Maint	Maintenance
APC	armored personnel carrier	Mech	mechanized
Armd	Armored	MG	machine gun
Arty	Artillery	MI	Military Intelligence
ARVN	Army of the Republic of Vietnam	MP	Military Police
ASA	Army Security Agency	NCO	noncommissioned officer
AVLB	armored vehicle-launched bridge	NVA	North Vietnamese Army
Avn	Aviation	OPCON	operational control
Bde	Brigade	Plat	Platoon
Bn	Battalion	Prov	Provisional
Btry	Battery	ROAD	Reorganization Objective Army Division
Cav	Cavalry		
Cbt	Combat	RON	remain overnight
CO	commanding officer	RTO	radio-telephone operator
Co	Company	Sep	Separate
CP	command post	SP	self-propelled
CSC	Combat Support Company	Sqdn	Squadron
CTZ	Corps Tactical Zone	TAOR	Tactical Area of Responsibility
Det	Detachment	TC	tank or track commander
DISCOM	Division Support Command	TDY	temporary duty
Div	Division	TO&E	Table of Organization and Equipment
DIVARTY	Division Artillery	Trp	Troop
EM	enlisted men	USARV	US Army, Vietnam
FFV	Field Force, Vietnam	VC	Viet Cong
HHC/B/T/D	Headquarters and Headquarters Company/Battery/Troop/Detachment	WO	warrant officer
		XO	executive officer (second-in-command)

Index

References to illustrations and tables are shown in **bold**.